Visionaries

Jamestown's Critical Reading Program

Visionaries

15 Stories of Invention, Innovation, and Inspiration—with Exercises for Developing Reading Comprehension and Critical Thinking Skills

McGraw Hill Education

Bothell, WA • Chicago, IL • Columbus, OH • New York, NY

mheonline.com

 **Education**

Send all inquiries to:
McGraw-Hill Education
130 E. Randolph, Suite 400
Chicago, IL 60601

ISBN: 978-0-07-659072-8
MHID: 0-07-659072-0

Printed in the United States of America.

1 2 3 4 5 6 7 8 9 QDB 15 14 13 12 11

Contents

Unit Three

To the Student

Think about a time when something that was puzzling you suddenly made a lot of sense. Maybe you were looking for an answer to a problem. Maybe something you were doing or something you saw triggered an idea for a way to do something better, more quickly, or with less effort.

Everyone gets a good idea from time to time. Anyone can *dream*. But a visionary can make that dream come true—and it often comes true in the face of great odds and active resistance. The visionaries you will read about in this book were trying to create change. They were seeking to make the world better, more efficient, or more fun. They built things, changed society's rhythms, brought relief to the suffering, and made us see ourselves and our place in the world from a new perspective. They saw a way to do things differently, and they believed in themselves and their vision enough to try and make it happen.

In this book you will read about inventors, artists, scientists, and others who took bold and courageous action. Visionaries make windmills from spare parts and find new medicines. They connect oceans, wrap canyons in fabric, shape new rhythms, and create speech with a wave of the hand. These ideas came from people with open minds. Each story is a new adventure in the ways in which ideas make the leap from dreams to reality.

As you read and enjoy the articles, you will also develop your reading skills. *Visionaries* is for students who already read fairly well but who want to read faster and to increase their understanding of what they read. If you complete the 15 lessons—reading the articles and completing the exercises—you will surely increase your reading speed and improve your reading comprehension and critical thinking skills. Also, because these exercises include items of the types often found on state and national tests, you will find that learning how to complete them will prepare you for tests you may have to take in the future.

How to Use This Book

About the Book. *Visionaries* contains three units, each of which includes five lessons. Each lesson begins with an article about a unique event, person, or group. The article is followed by a group of four reading comprehension exercises and a set of three critical thinking exercises. The reading comprehension exercises will help you understand the article. The critical thinking exercises will help you think about what you have read and how it relates to your own experience.

At the end of each lesson, you will also have the opportunity to give your personal response to some aspect of the article and then to assess how well you understood what you read.

The Sample Lesson. Working through the sample lesson, the first lesson in the book, with your class or group will demonstrate how a lesson is organized. The sample lesson explains how to complete the exercises and score your answers. The correct answers for the sample exercises and sample scores are printed in lighter type. In some cases, explanations of the correct answers are given. The explanations will help you understand how to think through these question types.

If you have any questions about how to complete the exercises or score them, this is the time to get the answers.

Working Through Each Lesson. Begin each lesson by looking at the photographs and reading the captions. Before you read, predict what you think the article will be about. Then read the article.

Sometimes your teacher may decide to time your reading. Timing helps you keep track of and increase your reading speed. If you have been timed, enter your reading time in the box at the end of the article. Then use the Words-per-Minute Table to find your reading speed, and record your speed on the Reading Speed graph at the end of the unit.

Next, complete the Reading Comprehension and Critical Thinking exercises. The directions for each exercise will tell you how to mark your answers. When you have finished all four Reading Comprehension exercises, use the answer key provided by your teacher to check your work. Follow the directions after each exercise to find your score. Record your Reading Comprehension scores on the graph at the end of each unit. Then check your answers to the Author's Approach, Summarizing and Paraphrasing, and Critical Thinking exercises. Fill in the Critical Thinking chart at the end of each unit with your evaluation of your work and comments about your progress.

At the end of each unit you will also complete a Compare and Contrast chart. The completed chart will help you see what the articles have in common. It will also give you an opportunity to explore your thoughts and feelings about the people we call visionaries.

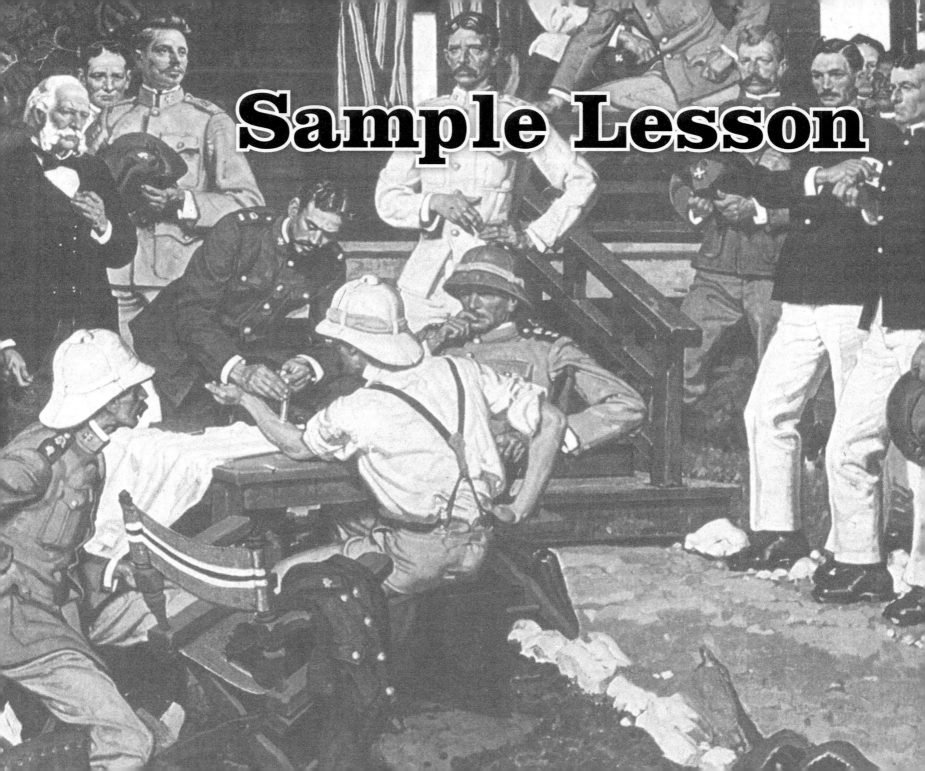

Dr. Finlay's Fever Dream

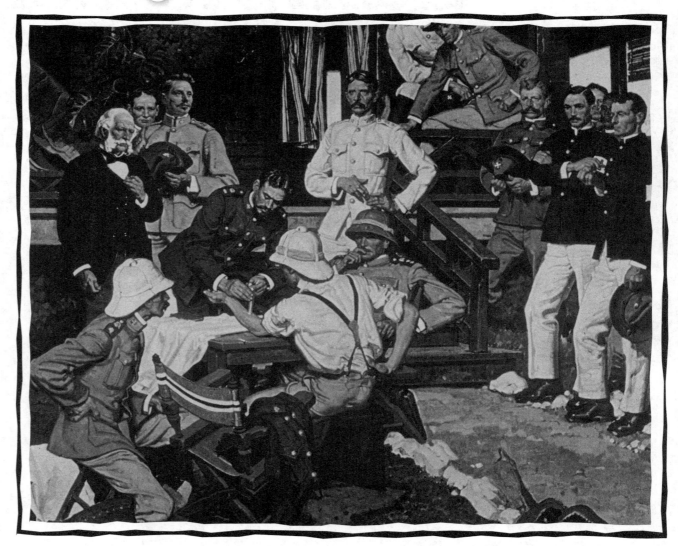

Dr. Jesse Lazear injects a volunteer with the blood of someone who had yellow fever to prove that the disease was in the blood.

His name was Dr. Carlos Juan Finlay, but many of his colleagues called him "The Mosquito Man." Others had less polite names for him—"crank" or even "crazy old man." Everyone, it seemed, thought this Cuban doctor had made a complete fool of himself during his 1881 presentation to Havana's Academy of Science. They said Finlay's theory was wild and completely contrary to common sense. Yet Finlay was sure he was right. He knew he had figured out how yellow fever was spread. Now he just needed a way to *prove* it.

2 Yellow fever is no joke. This disease begins with fever and muscle pain and often is accompanied by headache, chills, loss of appetite, and vomiting. After three or four days, these symptoms disappear. If a person is lucky, that is the end of it. But in many victims, the disease goes on to a second, more deadly stage. The fever returns, along with severe pain in the abdomen. As dangerous substances build up in the patient's bloodstream, the skin turns a sickly shade of yellow. Soon the afflicted person begins to bleed from the mouth, nose, and eyes. At that point, the patient has only a 50-50 chance of survival.

3 Today there is a vaccine that will cure or prevent yellow fever, but this vaccine was not developed until the 1930s. Before then, medicine was useless against the illness. From 1668 to 1893 there were more than 500 widespread outbreaks of yellow fever in cities across North America. In 1878 more than 20,000 people died in Louisiana,

Mississippi, and Tennessee. Then, beginning in 1890, a series of three epidemics of the fever crept through Philadelphia and killed almost 10 percent of the population. One of the most common treatments for fevers in those days was bloodletting, which involved opening a patient's veins and letting the "bad blood" drain out. Doctors also frequently attempted to keep patients cool by wrapping them in blankets soaked in vinegar.

4 The 1880 Annual Report of the National Board of Health blamed Cuba for the spread of yellow fever. It claimed that the island country just 90 miles from Florida was a great "nursery and camping ground" of yellow fever. The report said the disease was spread from this country "as from a central hell." But while everyone knew how dangerous the disease could be, no one was sure what caused it. Most people believed it was spread in two ways: through direct contact with an infected person and through contact with an infected person's personal items, such as clothing, dishes, and books.

5 Carlos Finlay had a different idea. He knew that some who had studied yellow fever had guessed that insects were responsible for spreading the disease. Finlay thought

these people were correct. When the United States created its Yellow Fever Commission of 1879, Finlay was one of the Cuban scientists chosen. The work Finlay did as part of this commission convinced him he was on the right track. Looking at microscopic bits of body tissue from yellow fever victims, Finlay found traces of the disease in the walls of the blood vessels. From this, he

Dr. Walter Reed confirmed Finlay's theory about yellow fever.

concluded that the disease was spreading directly from the blood of one person to the blood of another. The most likely cause, he decided, was a common mosquito in Cuba, the *Aedes aegypti*.

6   On August 14, 1881, Finlay presented his theory to Havana's Academy of Science. Finlay knew what he was up against. He fully expected the scientists gathered for the presentation to ridicule his theory—and they did. After all, how could such a tiny insect, a common little bug, cause such widespread illness and suffering?

7   Instead of dismissing the question, Finlay set out to answer it. He decided to prove his theory with a series of experiments. For the next 20 years he conducted one test after another. Finlay's experiments involved breeding his own mosquitoes and feeding them on blood from yellow fever victims. Then he set these mosquitoes free in a room to bite human volunteers. He hoped the volunteers would come down with a mild form of yellow fever from which they could recover easily. Studies had shown that people who had recovered from yellow fever appeared to become immune to the virus. Finlay hoped to create immunity against yellow fever while at the same time proving that the mosquito had caused the disease. However, Finlay's results were not consistent. Some volunteers got sick from his mosquitoes, but many others did not.

8   In the meantime, the medical community was beginning to change its opinion of

Finlay's theory. In 1900 Dr. Walter Reed was put in charge of a U.S Army Yellow Fever Board to study causes of the disease. Reed and other board members came to see Finlay, and the men discussed his experiments and studied his findings. Finlay agreed to let Reed use his homegrown mosquitoes to run a new series of tests.

9   Reed put 34-year-old Jesse Lazear in charge of the new tests, which began in August of 1900. Lazear exposed 11 separate volunteers to mosquitoes that had been fed with blood from yellow fever victims. Some of the volunteers were members of the Yellow Fever Board; the rest were soldiers who bravely offered to help. The first nine volunteers remained perfectly healthy. For the last two, however, Lazear used older mosquitoes. In those two cases, nearly two weeks had passed from the time the mosquitoes ingested the diseased blood until the time they bit the volunteers. It was this delay that did the trick. Both of these last two volunteers came down with yellow fever.

10   Lazear had discovered the final piece to the puzzle of how yellow fever was spread. He had proven that Carlos Finlay's theory was correct. What Finlay didn't know—and what Lazear showed—was that the disease needed 10 days to develop inside a mosquito before it could be spread to humans. Because Finlay had never waited that long, his experiments had failed, but his reasoning about the way the disease was transmitted was exactly right.

11   Lazear did not live long enough to enjoy his success. Within a month, he came down with yellow fever and died. Many historians believe that he had used himself as an unofficial 12th volunteer, although there is no direct proof of this. Dr. Walter Reed carried on Lazear's work, showing that mosquitoes could pick up the disease only in the first three days of its course. In the United States, Reed was given credit for stopping the epidemic. However, he said, "It was Finlay's theory, and he deserves much for having suggested it."

12   With his theory proven at last, Finlay became an important medical presence in Cuba. After years of ridicule and scorn, this visionary doctor had at last been proven correct. ✳

If you have been timed while reading this article, enter your reading time below. Then turn to the Words-per-Minute Table on page 55 and look up your reading speed (words per minute). Enter your reading speed on the graph on page 56.

Reading Time: Sample Lesson

_____ : _____
    Minutes   *Seconds*

A Finding the Main Idea

One statement below expresses the main idea of the article. One statement is too general, or too broad. The other statement explains only part of the article; it is too narrow. Label the statements using the following key:

M—Main Idea   B—Too Broad   N—Too Narrow

___B___ 1. Dr. Carlos Juan Finlay of Cuba was recognized as a leading expert on the spread of yellow fever. [This statement is true, but it is *too broad*. It does not describe his theory about how yellow fever was spread or the efforts needed to prove it.]

___M___ 2. At first ridiculed for his theory, Dr. Carlos Juan Finlay concluded that yellow fever is spread through mosquito bites and was eventually proven correct. [This statement is the *main idea*. It tells you that the article describes Dr. Finlay's theory and states that at first it was not accepted but then was proven to be true.]

___N___ 3. Dr. Carlos Juan Finlay was the first to suggest that yellow fever was spread by mosquitoes, not by contact with diseased people or their belongings. [This statement is true, but it is *too narrow*. This statement mentions only a few details from the article.]

___15___ Score 15 points for a correct M answer.

___10___ Score 5 points for each correct B or N answer.

___25___ **Total Score:** Finding the Main Idea

B Recalling Facts

How well do you remember the facts in the article? Put an X in the box next to the answer that correctly completes each statement about the article.

1. Symptoms of yellow fever include
  ☐ a. loss of memory, confusion, and intense thirst.
  ☒ b. headache, chills, vomiting, and bleeding.
  ☐ c. intense hunger, hot flashes, and excitement.

2. Widespread outbreaks of yellow fever in the United States
  ☐ a. were all mild and did not kill anyone.
  ☐ b. were almost unheard of.
  ☒ c. occurred hundreds of times from 1668 to 1893.

3. Dr. Finlay first presented his yellow fever theory in
  ☒ a. 1881.
  ☐ b. 1890.
  ☐ c. 1879.

4. In 1900 Dr. Walter Reed was put in charge of
  ☒ a. a board that studied yellow fever.
  ☐ b. the only hospital that treated victims of yellow fever.
  ☐ c. Dr. Finlay.

5. Jesse Lazear proved that yellow fever
  ☐ a. could be transmitted to a mosquito only in the first three days of its course.
  ☒ b. needed 10 days to develop inside a mosquito before the mosquito could spread it to another victim.
  ☐ c. could be spread by sneezes or coughs.

Score 5 points for each correct answer.

___25___ **Total Score:** Recalling Facts

C Making Inferences

When you combine your own experiences and information from a text to draw a conclusion that is not directly stated in that text, you are making an inference. Below are five statements that may or may not be inferences based on information in the article. Label the statements using the following key:

C—Correct Inference   **F—Faulty Inference**

__C__ 1. In 1900, yellow fever was an important public health problem. [This is a *correct* inference. A government board was commissioned just to study the disease.]

__F__ 2. New theories about medicine and science are accepted without much discussion. [This is a *faulty* inference. Dr. Finlay and others worked for years before his theory was accepted.]

__F__ 3. Jesse Lazear's volunteers did not realize that they could get yellow fever. [This is a *faulty* inference. They were described as brave, so they must have known the risks.]

__F__ 4. Only U.S. citizens ever are asked to serve on American scientific commissions. [This is a *faulty* inference. Dr. Finlay, a Cuban, served on the 1879 Yellow Fever Commission.]

__C__ 5. Keeping good records was essential for discovering how yellow fever is spread. [This is a *correct* inference. Lazear's records showed which volunteers were exposed to older mosquitoes.]

Score 5 points for each correct answer.

__25__ **Total Score:** Making Inferences

D Using Words Precisely

Each numbered sentence below contains an underlined word or phrase from the article. Following the sentence are three definitions. One definition is closest to the meaning of the underlined word. One definition is opposite or nearly opposite. Label those two definitions using the following key. Do not label the remaining definition.

C—Closest   **O—Opposite or Nearly Opposite**

1. Soon the <u>afflicted</u> person begins to bleed from the mouth, nose, and even the eyes.
   __O__ a. healthy
   __C__ b. badly affected by disease
   _____ c. surprised

2. A series of three <u>epidemics</u> of the fever crept through Philadelphia and killed almost 10 percent of the population.
   __O__ a. medicines for treating sickness
   _____ b. health workers
   __C__ c. outbreaks of diseases that spread quickly

3. Studies had shown that people who had recovered from yellow fever appeared to become <u>immune to</u> the virus.
   __O__ a. likely to become sickened by
   __C__ b. protected from
   _____ c. excited by

4. In those two cases, nearly two weeks had passed from the time the mosquitoes <u>ingested</u> the diseased blood until the time they bit the volunteers.
   __O__ a. spit out
   _____ b. recommended
   __C__ c. taken in as food

5. Finlay's reasoning about the way the disease was <u>transmitted</u> was exactly right.

_____ a. left wide open

_C_ b. sent or spread from one person or place to another

_O_ c. contained in one person or place

_15_ Score 3 points for each correct C answer.

_10_ Score 2 points for each correct O answer.

_25_ **Total Score**: Using Words Precisely

Enter the four total scores in the spaces below, and add them together to find your Reading Comprehension Score. Then record your score on the graph on page 57.

Score	Question Type	Sample Lesson
25	Finding the Main Idea	
25	Recalling Facts	
25	Making Inferences	
25	Using Words Precisely	
100	**Reading Comprehension Score**	

Author's Approach

Put an X in the box next to the correct answer.

1. The main purpose of the first paragraph is to

☒ a. show that Dr. Finlay's theory was not accepted at first.

☐ b. explain the link between mosquitoes and yellow fever.

☐ c. describe Dr. Carlos Juan Finlay's personality.

2. From the statements below, choose the one that you believe the author would agree with.

☐ a. Dr. Finlay cared too much about what other people said about him.

☐ b. Dr. Finlay could have proven his theory without help.

☒ c. Dr. Finlay was intelligent, self-confident, and persistent.

3. Choose the statement below that best describes the author's position in paragraph 11.

☒ a. It was appropriate that Dr. Reed gave Dr. Finlay much of the credit for stopping the spread of yellow fever.

☐ b. Dr. Reed was just being modest; he deserves most of the credit for stopping the spread of yellow fever.

☐ c. If Lazear really used himself as the 12th volunteer, he deserves all the credit for stopping the spread of yellow fever.

4. The author probably wrote this article in order to

☐ a. persuade readers to avoid mosquitoes.

☒ b. tell the story of a man who discovered something new and useful.

☐ c. show how difficult it is to prove scientific theories.

_4_ Number of correct answers

Record your personal assessment of your work on the Critical Thinking Chart on page 58.

Summarizing and Paraphrasing

Follow the directions provided for question 1. Put an X in the box next to the correct answer for question 2.

1. Complete the following one-sentence summary of the article using the lettered phrases from the phrase bank below. Write the letters on the lines.

> **Phrase Bank:**
> a. how Finlay's theory was proven correct
> b. the scorn and ridicule heaped on Dr. Finlay for his theory
> c. how dangerous yellow fever was

The article, "Dr. Finlay's Fever Dream" begins with ___b___, goes on to describe ___c___, and ends with ___a___.

2. Below are summaries of the article. Choose the summary that says all the most important things about the article but in the fewest words.

☐ a. In spite of being ridiculed for his theory, Dr. Carlos Juan Finlay was finally proven to be correct. [This summary leaves out important information.]

☒ b. Dr. Carlos Juan Finlay, at first was scorned for his theory about the connection between mosquitoes and yellow fever, but was proven correct after years of experiments. [This summary says all the most important things about the article in the fewest words.]

☐ c. Dr. Carlos Juan Finlay was a Cuban doctor who believed that mosquitoes spread yellow fever, a deadly disease for which there was no effective treatment. Other doctors ridiculed him when he presented his theory to them at a conference in Havana, but he refused to give up. [This summary uses too many words and still leaves out important information.]

> ___2___ Number of correct answers
>
> Record your personal assessment of your work on the Critical Thinking Chart on page 58.

Critical Thinking

Follow the directions provided for questions 1 and 3. Put an X next to the correct answer for the other questions.

1. For each statement below, write O if it expresses an opinion or write F if it expresses a fact.

___O___ a. Yellow fever was the most painful and frightening disease known to mankind. [This statement is an *opinion*; it cannot be proved.]

___F___ b. A vaccine to protect against yellow fever was developed in the 1930s. [This statement is a *fact*; it can be proved.]

___F___ c. Dr. Carlos Juan Finlay served on the U.S. Yellow Fever Commission of 1879. [This statement is a *fact*; it can be proved.]

2. From the article, you can predict that if Dr. Finlay had been successful today, he would be

☐ a. running for political office in Cuba.

☐ b. unlikely to accept new ideas.

☒ c. trying to learn more about today's diseases.

3. Reread paragraph 5. Then choose from the letters below to correctly complete the following statement. Write the letters on the lines.

According to paragraph 5, ___b___ because ___a___.

a. Dr. Finlay noticed that the walls of blood vessels of yellow fever victims showed evidence of the disease

b. Dr. Finlay concluded that yellow fever spreads from the blood of one person to the blood of another

c. Dr. Finlay was invited to serve on the Yellow Fever Commission

4. What did you have to do to answer question 3?

☒ a. find a cause (why something happened)

☐ b. find an opinion (what someone thinks about something)

☐ c. find a comparison (how things are the same)

_____4_____ Number of correct answers

Record your personal assessment of your work on the Critical Thinking Chart on page 58.

Personal Response

I can't believe . . .

[Record any idea or action described in the article that

shocked or surprised you or that you found difficult to believe.]

_____

_____

_____

_____

_____

Self-Assessment

Before reading this article, I already knew

[List any ideas found in the article with which you were already

familiar. For example, had you ever heard of yellow fever before?

Had you heard the names of any of the people mentioned here?

Were you aware of the dangers of mosquito bites?]

_____

_____

_____

_____

_____

_____

_____

_____

_____

CRITICAL THINKING

Self-Assessment

To get the most out of the *Above & Beyond* series, you need to take charge of your own progress in improving your reading comprehension and critical thinking skills. Here are some of the features that help you work on those essential skills.

Reading Comprehension Exercises. Complete these exercises immediately after reading the article. They help you recall what you have read, understand the stated and implied main ideas, and add words to your working vocabulary.

Critical Thinking Skills Exercises. These exercises help you focus on the author's approach and purpose, recognize and generate summaries and paraphrases, and identify relationships between ideas.

Personal Response and Self-Assessment. Questions in this category help you relate the articles to your personal experience and give you the opportunity to evaluate your understanding of the information in that lesson.

Compare and Contrast Charts. At the end of each unit you will complete a Compare and Contrast chart. The completed chart helps you see what the articles have in common and gives you an opportunity to explore your own ideas about the topics discussed in the articles.

The Graphs. The graphs and charts at the end of each unit enable you to keep track of your progress. Check your graphs regularly with your teacher. Decide whether your progress is satisfactory or whether you need additional work on some skills. What types of exercises are you having difficulty with? Talk with your teacher about ways to work on the skills in which you need the most practice.

Unit One

The Boy Who Powered a Village

William Kamkwamba built an electricity-producing windmill from trash.

For most of 2002, 14-year-old William Kamkwamba's life looked pretty bleak. He had not done well on his school tests. That meant he had no chance of getting into one of the better high schools in his native country of Malawi in Africa. As a result, he had to attend the community high school in the town of Kasunga, a few miles from his rural village of Masitala. Worse than that, a severe drought had dried out the region, resulting in a famine that had killed thousands of Malawians. Kamkwamba's own family was barely surviving, teetering at times on the brink of starvation. Could things get worse?

2   The answer is yes, they could. Later that year, Kamkwamba learned his family could not afford the $80 annual tuition to send him to the community school. He would have to drop out. Kamkwamba didn't want to leave his classes, so he kept going to school. He dodged administrators for a few weeks until he was caught and sent home. Sick with hunger and terribly sad, Kamkwamba went out into the fields to help his family on their struggling maize and tobacco farm.

3   With no hope that his family could pay the tuition money, Kamkwamba decided to educate himself as best he could. He started borrowing books from a small library at his old elementary school. These books had been donated by a U.S.-backed organization called the Malawian Teacher Training Activity (MTTA). One day Kamkwamba picked up a tattered 8th-grade American science textbook titled *Using Energy*. One section described how windmills can be used to pump water from underground and to generate electricity.

4   Kamkwamba began to dream of bringing electricity to his family's homestead, which consisted of a few brick buildings perched on a hill overlooking Masitala. At the time, only 2 percent of the people in Malawi had electricity in their homes. As he later said, "I was very interested when I saw the windmill could make electricity and pump water." A windmill that could produce electricity would mean that people could read at night after work. A windmill that could pump water would mean that people would not have to spend two hours a day hauling water. It might allow them to grow two crops a year instead of just one. Kamkwamba thought, "That could be a defense against hunger. Maybe I should build one for myself." When he was not working in the field, he kept busy building a windmill. Because there was no electricity in his home, he worked by the light of a kerosene lamp, which gave off only a smoky and flickering light.

5   When word got around Masitala that young Kamkwamba wanted to build his own windmill, everyone, including his parents, thought he was out of his mind. "At first, we were laughing at him," said his mother. "We thought he was doing something useless." In part, this was because the two hundred or so villagers had never seen a windmill before, and they didn't understand what it might do. They were even more perplexed when Kamkwamba began to scour the rubbish piles and trash cans looking for materials with which to build his windmill. "So I told them I was only making something for magic. Then they said: 'Ah, I see.'"

6   Everyone in the village was absolutely astonished in 2002 when William Kamkwamba unveiled his windmill. He had lacked the necessary materials to make a water-pumping windmill, so he had

Kamkwamba now helps to run a project that builds primary schools in developing countries.

concentrated on building one that would provide electricity instead. He made his device out of possibly the oddest collection of materials ever assembled. The miscellany included slime-clogged PVC pipes, a broken bicycle, an old fan blade from a tractor, and a shock absorber. He could not afford to buy even a few nuts and bolts, and the only tools he had were a couple of wrenches. For a soldering iron, he used a piece of wire heated over a fire. Despite these limitations, Kamkwamba built a 16-foot frame from the wood of blue gum trees. On top of the frame was his dream machine, his windmill.

7   And the amazing thing was—it worked! One day in front of a crowd of unbelieving villagers, he hooked up a car light bulb to his turbine. As the blades began to whirl in the breeze, the bulb flickered to life and then glowed brightly. The astonished villagers broke into wild cheers.

8   With his new power source, Kamkwamba wired his house for four light bulbs and two radios. He installed his own on/off switches made from rubber sandals and bicycle spokes. He also rigged up a circuit breaker using nails and magnets off of an old stereo speaker. The breaker helped ensure that the thatched roof of his house did not catch fire. Over the next few years, Kamkwamba made some modifications to the windmill's design. For one thing, he

increased the number of blades from three to four to increase the output of power.

9   Kamkwamba and his windmill remained a local curiosity until 2006. That's when the deputy director of the MTTA, Dr. Hartford Mchazime, came to the village and saw it with his own eyes. As Mchazime listened to the story, he recognized right away what Kamkwamba had done. The story of the boy who brought electric power to his African village spread like hot gossip all around the world. Newspaper articles, blog posts, radio stories, and television appearances praised this new prodigy.

10   Kamkwamba was invited to Tanzania to give a presentation of his project at a science and culture conference called TED. He received a standing ovation from the guests there. The sophisticated setting was a real eye-opener for a young man from a remote village. It was the first time in his life he had seen a laptop computer, slept in a hotel on a real mattress, or felt the cool comfort of air conditioning.

11   Kamkwamba's modesty and winning personality won the high-tech audience. They willingly funded his efforts to build better windmills in his village. Over the next several years, Kamkwamba upgraded his original windmill. He anchored it in concrete after its wooden base was chewed away by termites, and he installed a solar-powered mechanical pump that brought

fresh water to the region around his village. He even built another windmill, which he called the Green Machine, to pump water that would irrigate his family's field. Meanwhile, well-wishers donated tuition money so that he could return to school. After being away from the classroom for more than five years, he enrolled in the highly ranked African Leadership Academy in Johannesburg, South Africa.

12   Kamkwamba took success in stride. He has upgraded his goal, and now wants to bring power to all of Malawi. "I want to help my country and apply the knowledge I've learned," he says. "I feel there's a lot of work to be done." ✳

If you have been timed while reading this article, enter your reading time below. Then turn to the Words-per-Minute Table on page 55 and look up your reading speed (words per minute). Enter your reading speed on the graph on page 56.

Reading Time: Lesson 1

_____ : _____
Minutes   *Seconds*

A Finding the Main Idea

One statement below expresses the main idea of the article. One statement is too general, or too broad. The other statement explains only part of the article; it is too narrow. Label the statements using the following key:

M—Main Idea   **B—Too Broad**   **N—Too Narrow**

_____ 1. With enough ability and determination, even a 14-year-old boy can make a difference in improving his community.

_____ 2. William Kamkwamba educated himself by reading books from a small library at his old school.

_____ 3. William Kamkwamba, a 14-year old boy in Malawi, Africa, built a windmill out of scrap materials to bring electricity to his family's home.

_____ Score 15 points for a correct M answer.

_____ Score 5 points for each correct B or N answer.

_____ **Total Score**: Finding the Main Idea

B Recalling Facts

How well do you remember the facts in the article? Put an X in the box next to the answer that correctly completes each statement about the article.

1. Kamkwamba's home was in the village of
   ☐ a. Masitala.
   ☐ b. Kasunga.
   ☐ c. Tanzania.

2. The first item that Kamkwamba's windmill powered was a
   ☐ a. radio.
   ☐ b. water pump.
   ☐ c. car light bulb.

3. At first, the only tools Kamkwamba had were
   ☐ a. a few hammers.
   ☐ b. a couple of wrenches.
   ☐ c. two screwdrivers.

4. Kamkwamba built a windmill that he called the Green Machine to
   ☐ a. bring water to the entire region around his village.
   ☐ b. provide electricity to his whole village.
   ☐ c. pump water to irrigate his family's field.

5. Kamkwamba entered the African Leadership Academy in
   ☐ a. South Africa.
   ☐ b. Tanzania.
   ☐ c. Malawi.

Score 5 points for each correct answer.

_____ **Total Score**: Recalling Facts

C Making Inferences

When you combine your own experiences and information from a text to draw a conclusion that is not directly stated in that text, you are making an inference. Below are five statements that may or may not be inferences based on information in the article. Label the statements using the following key:

C—Correct Inference   F—Faulty Inference

_____ 1. There were no free public high schools near Kamkwamba's village.

_____ 2. Now that Kamkwamba has become famous, he has also become rich.

_____ 3. Today every village in Malawi has a windmill.

_____ 4. The villagers who lived near Kamkwamba were not highly educated.

_____ 5. The people in Kamkwamba's village were very poor.

Score 5 points for each correct answer.

_____ **Total Score**: Making Inferences

D Using Words Precisely

Each numbered sentence below contains an underlined word or phrase from the article. Following the sentence are three definitions. One definition is closest to the meaning of the underlined word. One definition is opposite or nearly opposite. Label those two definitions using the following key. Do not label the remaining definition.

C—Closest   O—Opposite or Nearly Opposite

1. In 2002 William Kamkwamba's life looked <u>bleak</u>.
   _____ a. cheerful, pleasant
   _____ b. depressing, hopeless
   _____ c. busy, active

2. The villagers were <u>perplexed</u> when Kamkwamba began to scour the rubbish piles and trash cans.
   _____ a. supportive, helpful
   _____ b. understanding, comprehending
   _____ c. puzzled, bewildered

3. The <u>miscellany</u> included slime-clogged PVC pipes, a broken bicycle, an old fan blade from a tractor, and a shock absorber.
   _____ a. a collection of same or similar things
   _____ b. mixture, assortment
   _____ c. material

4. Over the next few years, Kamkwamba made some <u>modifications</u> to the windmill's design.
   _____ a. extreme makeovers
   _____ b. responses
   _____ c. alterations, minor changes

5. Newspaper articles, blog posts, radio stories, and television appearances praised this new <u>prodigy</u>.

_____ a. highly talented, intelligent young person

_____ b. person who does not succeed

_____ c. fashionable, fast-talking character

_____ Score 3 points for each correct C answer.

_____ Score 2 points for each correct O answer.

_____ **Total Score**: Using Words Precisely

Enter the four total scores in the spaces below, and add them together to find your Reading Comprehension Score. Then record your score on the graph on page 57.

Score	Question Type	Lesson 1
_____	Finding the Main Idea	
_____	Recalling Facts	
_____	Making Inferences	
_____	Using Words Precisely	
_____	**Reading Comprehension Score**	

Author's Approach

Put an X in the box next to the correct answer.

1. The main purpose of the first paragraph is to
   ☐ a. introduce the reader to William Kamkwamba.
   ☐ b. explain how drought affected Kamkwamba's country.
   ☐ c. give some information about schools in Malawi.

2. The author probably wrote this article to
   ☐ a. inform the reader about conditions in Malawi.
   ☐ b. tell an inspiring story about a creative, intelligent boy.
   ☐ c. encourage readers to study science.

3. Judging by statements from the article "The Boy Who Powered a Village," you can conclude that the author wants the reader to think that
   ☐ a. Kamkwamba is more famous outside of Malawi than he is in his own country.
   ☐ b. the people of Malawi are proud of Kamkwamba and his work.
   ☐ c. Kamkwamba only built the windmill as a way to go to a better school and leave Malawi.

4. In this article, "Kamkwamba took success in stride" means
   ☐ a. Kamkwamba responded to the praise he received by walking away purposefully.
   ☐ b. Kamkwamba achieved success by following a steady pace.
   ☐ c. Kamkwamba dealt with his success easily and without changing.

_____ Number of correct answers

Record your personal assessment of your work on the Critical Thinking Chart on page 58.

Summarizing and Paraphrasing

Follow the directions provided for questions 1 and 3. Put an X in the box next to the correct answer for question 2.

1. Complete the following one-sentence summary of the article using the lettered phrases from the phrase bank below. Write the letters on the lines.

> **Phrase Bank:**
> a. Kamkwamba making a windmill in his village
> b. Kamkwamba hoping to bring power to his whole country
> c. Kamkwamba not doing well on his school tests

The article, "The Boy Who Powered a Village" begins with _____, goes on to describe _____, and ends with _____.

2. Read the statement from the article below. Then read the paraphrase of that statement. Choose the reason that best tells why the paraphrase does not say the same thing as the statement.

Statement: As the blades began to whirl in the breeze, the bulb flickered to life and then glowed brightly. The astonished villagers broke into wild cheers.

Paraphrase: The people of the village were surprised that the windmill actually worked.

☐ a. Paraphrase says too much.
☐ b. Paraphrase doesn't say enough.
☐ c. Paraphrase doesn't agree with the statement.

3. Look for the important ideas and events in paragraphs 3 and 4. Summarize those paragraphs in one or two sentences.

_____

_____

_____

_____

> _____ Number of correct answers
>
> Record your personal assessment of your work on the Critical Thinking Chart on page 58.

Critical Thinking

Follow the directions provided for questions 1, 3, and 5. Put an X in the box next to the correct answer for the other questions.

1. For each statement below, write O if it expresses an opinion or write F if it expresses a fact.

_____ a. The introduction of electricity was the best improvement ever made in Kamkwamba's village.

_____ b. William Kamkwamba finished his first windmill in 2002.

_____ c. Kamkwamba's cleverest invention was the on/off switch made from rubber sandals and bicycle spokes.

2. From what the article told about William Kamkwamba, you can predict that

☐ a. he would prefer to build something else rather than go to school.
☐ b. he will build only what pays him the most money.
☐ c. he will look for projects that will benefit poor people.

CRITICAL THINKING

3. Choose from the letters below to correctly complete the following statement. Write the letters on the lines.

According to the article, _____ caused the windmill to _____, and the effect was _____.

   a. the blades of the windmill turning in the breeze

   b. a lit light bulb

   c. generate electricity

4. From the information in paragraphs 6 and 8, you can conclude that

☐ a. Kamkwamba was surprised when his windmill worked.

☐ b. Kamkwamba did not have a very good idea of how to build a windmill.

☐ c. Kamkwamba was resourceful and able to see how to use common articles in an inventive way.

5. In which paragraph did you find your information or details to answer question 3?

_____

_____ Number of correct answers

Record your personal assessment of your work on the Critical Thinking Chart on page 58.

Personal Response

What would you do if you were not able to attend school?

_____

_____

_____

_____

Self-Assessment

From reading this article I have learned

_____

_____

_____

_____

_____

_____

_____

_____

_____

_____

CRITICAL THINKING

Musical Noise

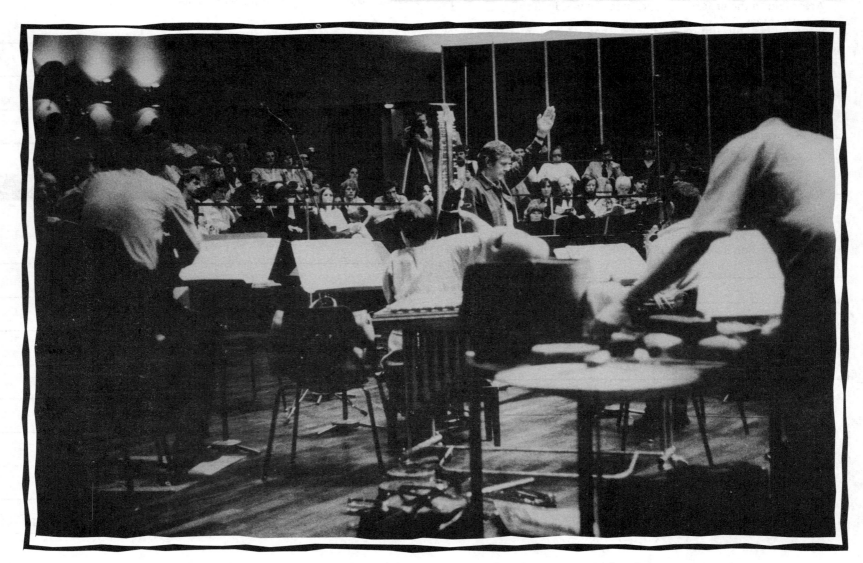

Cage conducts his compostion Atlas Eclipticalis, *in which a collection of 103 instruments plays their own series of single tones.*

It was August 29, 1952, and the people who filed into the open-air Maverick Concert Hall near Woodstock, New York, knew the music they were about to hear would be a bit different. After all, the composer was John Cage, a man with a reputation as a musical innovator. The concertgoers, all strong supporters of contemporary art, were eager to hear Cage's new work. It was a composition in three parts, or movements, called 4'33". The night was peaceful. The crowd politely settled into their seats as the sounds of the surrounding forest drifted through the air. At last David Tudor walked across the stage, acknowledged the audience's applause, and sat down at the piano. No one was prepared for what happened next.

2   Tudor opened Cage's hand-written score and then, to the audience's surprise, he *lowered* the lid of the keyboard. He pulled out a stopwatch and sat motionless for 30 seconds, the length of the first movement. He signaled the end of the movement by opening the keyboard lid. He then closed it again and quietly timed the next 2 minutes and 23 seconds, the length of the second movement. The score was several pages long, so Tudor did occasionally reach out and turn the pages, but he made no attempt to play the piano. Tudor repeated his actions for the final movement. This one lasted 1 minute and 40 seconds. For the entire length of the piece—a total of 4 minutes and 33 seconds—there was total silence.

3   Actually, "total silence" is not at all how John Cage would have described it. He believed that *silence* defined as "a total absence of sound" did not exist. There is always some sound. A year earlier, in 1951, he had visited a special chamber at Harvard University. This chamber was free from echoes or any background noises, so Cage expected silence. "I literally expected to hear nothing," he said. Instead, he heard two sounds, one high and one low. He was later told that the first sound was his nervous system, and the second was his blood circulating. The revelation that there is no such thing as absolute silence affected Cage's philosophy of music from that time on. To him, "Everything we do is music." It is in the environment. Said Cage, "It only stops when we turn away and stop paying attention."

4   Cage maintained that in the case of 4'33", there was plenty of sound. During the first movement, there was the sound of wind moving through the trees. In the second movement, raindrops fell on the roof of the hall. And during the third movement, some people in the audience began to mutter and complain, and others angrily stormed out.

5   That performance started a lot of discussion. Artists, lovers of experimental music, and people who wanted to discredit

John Cage believed music was everywhere and could be created from anything.

Cage all voiced their opinions. Anyone who had been aware of Cage's life and career should not have been shocked by 4'33". Cage had, in the words of his hero Henry David Thoreau, always marched to the beat of "a different drummer." Even Cage's high school yearbook said of him, "Noted for being radical." As a student at Pomona College, Cage scoffed at the fact that all students read the same assigned books. He registered his protest by declining to read an assigned text and choosing a different book instead. "I went into the stacks and read the first book written by an author whose name began with Z," he later recalled. Instead of writing a paper about the assigned book, he wrote about the book he had selected by chance.

6   Cage dropped out of college after two years. From then on, he concentrated full time on his music. He studied classical music, including solo piano, orchestra, and voice. Eventually he rejected them all in favor of sounds that were free from a composer's will. He started creating music that was random and unpredictable.

7   In a work titled "Imaginary Landscape No. 4," Cage used 12 radios, turned on to various stations at different volumes. The entire piece was governed totally by whatever happened to be on those radio stations at that time. In "Imaginary Landscape No. 5," he used 42 phonograph records in the same random way. In "Water Music," a musician was instructed not only to play the piano but also turn a radio on and off, shuffle playing cards, blow a duck whistle into a bowl of water, pour water from one glass into another, and slam shut the keyboard lid of the piano.

8   Cage explored ways to make new sounds. He created an instrument he called "the prepared piano" by placing a variety of objects, such as screws, bolts, and pieces of rubber between the strings of a grand piano. He played the instrument by plucking the piano strings. Cage meant to create a sound something like a one-person percussion orchestra.

9   Although there were random parts to Cage's works, they actually were composed with strict rules. Anyone who performs a John Cage composition has to follow his written instructions for making the sounds and also make the sounds in the proper way. Even so, Cage himself was not against changing his instructions in mid-performance. Once, for an appearance on a TV show, Cage had chosen to perform one of his works called "Water Walk." His one-man "orchestra" included a rubber duck, a bathtub, an electric mixer, and a number of radios. Cage learned just before the performance that the radios could not be turned on. He took the news in stride. At the correct moment he knocked them all onto the floor instead.

10   Until he died in 1992, Cage continued to enjoy listening to random sounds. "I couldn't be happier," he said late in his life, "than I am in this apartment, with the sounds from Sixth Avenue constantly surprising me, never once repeating themselves."

11   Cage's influence on the world of music will never be questioned, even though many still argue whether the sounds he created actually were music. Cage was elected to the Institute of the American Academy of Arts and Letters in 1968. He also received an honorary Doctorate of Performing Arts from the California Institute of the Arts in 1986. Cage wasn't satisfied with the boundaries that had been set for music—the accepted ideas of harmony, rhythm, and melody. Instead, he thought that music has many more possibilities, and he wanted people to listen to and appreciate the layers and textures that random sounds provide. For John Cage, everything was music to his ears. ✳

If you have been timed while reading this article, enter your reading time below. Then turn to the Words-per-Minute Table on page 55 and look up your reading speed (words per minute). Enter your reading speed on the graph on page 56.

Reading Time: Lesson 2

_____ : _____
Minutes   Seconds

A Finding the Main Idea

One statement below expresses the main idea of the article. One statement is too general, or too broad. The other statement explains only part of the article; it is too narrow. Label the statements using the following key:

M—Main Idea   **B—Too Broad**   **N—Too Narrow**

_____ 1. John Cage wrote music that explored the boundaries of both music and art with its random nature and use of unusual instruments.

_____ 2. John Cage was famous for his innovative approach to music.

_____ 3. Some of John Cage's music features the sounds of objects such as radios, duck whistles, rubber ducks, and electric mixers.

_____ Score 15 points for a correct M answer.

_____ Score 5 points for each correct B or N answer.

_____ **Total Score**: Finding the Main Idea

B Recalling Facts

How well do you remember the facts in the article? Put an X in the box next to the answer that correctly completes each statement about the article.

1. John Cage's 4'33" is 4 minutes and 33 seconds of
   - ☐ a. the sounds of electric mixers and whistles.
   - ☐ b. random sounds of radios turned on and off.
   - ☐ c. random sounds from the environment and the audience.

2. Cage's high school yearbook described him as
   - ☐ a. a talented musician.
   - ☐ b. radical.
   - ☐ c. unusual.

3. For two years, Cage attended
   - ☐ a. Harvard University.
   - ☐ b. Pomona College.
   - ☐ c. Berklee College of Music.

4. Cage knocked over radios during a performance because
   - ☐ a. his musician did not arrive.
   - ☐ b. he could not find a hammer.
   - ☐ c. he wasn't allowed to turn them on.

5. Cage made his "prepared piano" by
   - ☐ a. placing objects between the strings of a grand piano.
   - ☐ b. holding the strings of a grand piano perfectly still.
   - ☐ c. pouring water onto the strings of a grand piano.

Score 5 points for each correct answer.

_____ **Total Score**: Recalling Facts

C Making Inferences

When you combine your own experiences and information from a text to draw a conclusion that is not directly stated in that text, you are making an inference. Below are five statements that may or may not be inferences based on information in the article. Label the statements using the following key:

C—Correct Inference   **F—Faulty Inference**

_____ 1. John Cage could have written 4'33" for guitar or drums instead of for piano.

_____ 2. Each time you hear "Imaginary Landscape No. 4" played live, it could sound different.

_____ 3. Cage probably rejected his classical music education because he was not talented enough to perform it.

_____ 4. Cage was never really accepted by anyone in the art community.

_____ 5. To be an innovator, you sometimes have to ignore the opinions and advice of others.

Score 5 points for each correct answer.

_____ **Total Score**: Making Inferences

D Using Words Precisely

Each numbered sentence below contains an underlined word or phrase from the article. Following the sentence are three definitions. One definition is closest to the meaning of the underlined word. One definition is opposite or nearly opposite. Label those two definitions using the following key. Do not label the remaining definition.

C—Closest   **O—Opposite or Nearly Opposite**

1. The concertgoers, all strong supporters of <u>contemporary</u> art, were eager to hear Cage's new work, called 4'33".

_____ a. old-fashioned

_____ b. well-known

_____ c. modern

2. The <u>revelation</u> that there is no such thing as absolute silence affected Cage's philosophy of music from that time on.

_____ a. sorrow

_____ b. discovery

_____ c. secret

3. Artists, lovers of experimental music, and people who wanted to <u>discredit</u> Cage all voiced their opinions.

_____ a. understand

_____ b. ruin the reputation of

_____ c. praise

4. As a student, he <u>scoffed at</u> the fact that all students read the same assigned books.

_____ a. mocked

_____ b. appreciated

_____ c. expressed surprise at

5. Cage created music that was <u>random</u> and unpredictable.

_____ a. carefully thought out and planned

_____ b. beautiful

_____ c. without pattern; selected by chance

_____ Score 3 points for each correct C answer.

_____ Score 2 points for each correct O answer.

_____ **Total Score**: Using Words Precisely

Enter the four total scores in the spaces below, and add them together to find your Reading Comprehension Score. Then record your score on the graph on page 57.

Score	Question Type	Lesson 2
_____	Finding the Main Idea	
_____	Recalling Facts	
_____	Making Inferences	
_____	Using Words Precisely	
_____	**Reading Comprehension Score**	

Author's Approach

Put an X in the box next to the correct answer.

1. The author probably wrote this article in order to

☐ a. persuade readers to invent new ways of writing music.

☐ b. show that people who try new things are always more creative than those who prefer the old ways.

☐ c. tell the story of an artist who tried to show that music can take many forms.

2. Judging by statements from the article "Musical Noise" you can conclude that the author wants the reader to think that

☐ a. John Cage was not treated fairly by the music community.

☐ b. John Cage pursued his beliefs with a passion.

☐ c. John Cage tried to fool people into thinking he was writing music when he was simply making noise.

3. Considering the statement from the article "I couldn't be happier," he said late in his life, "than I am in this apartment, with the sounds from Sixth Avenue constantly surprising me, never once repeating themselves" you can conclude that the author wants the reader to think that Cage

☐ a. listened closely to sounds and enjoyed their random nature.

☐ b. wanted to record the street noise for his next concert.

☐ c. was glad to rest and let the world make noise.

4. The author probably told about Cage enjoying the street sounds from his open window in order to show that he

☐ a. never listened to anything but noise.

☐ b. lived in the city, where sounds are generally constant.

☐ c. enjoyed the sounds for their own sake, not just for performance.

5. What does the author mean by the statement "Everything we do is music. It is in the environment. It only stops when we turn away and stop paying attention."

☐ a. Cage believed if you do not listen to music, you cannot make music.

☐ b. For Cage, music could be any sounds, not just those made by a musician.

☐ c. Cage thinks that only the sounds that he makes are worthy of attention.

_____ Number of correct answers

Record your personal assessment of your work on the Critical Thinking Chart on page 58.

Summarizing and Paraphrasing

Put an X in the box next to the correct answer for questions 1 and 2. Follow the directions provided for question 3.

1. Choose the best one-sentence paraphrase for the following sentence from the article: "Cage took the news in stride. "

☐ a. Cage took the news hard.

☐ b. Cage accepted the news and it didn't bother him at all.

☐ c. Cage heard the news as he was walking away.

2. Read the statement about the article below. Then read the paraphrase of that statement. Choose the reason that best tells why the paraphrase does not say the same thing as the statement.

Statement: Instead of reading an assigned book, Cage chose a book at random from the library shelves.

Paraphrase: Objecting to an assignment that required all students to read the same book, Cage chose a book by an author whose name began with the letter Z instead.

☐ a. Paraphrase says too much.

☐ b. Paraphrase doesn't say enough.

☐ c. Paraphrase doesn't agree with the statement.

3. Reread paragraph 8 in the article. Below, write a summary of the paragraph in no more than 25 words.

_____

_____

_____

_____

_____

Reread your summary and decide whether it covers the important ideas in the paragraph. Next, decide how to shorten the summary to 15 words or less without leaving out any essential information. Write this summary below.

_____

_____

_____

_____

_____

_____ Number of correct answers

Record your personal assessment of your work on the Critical Thinking Chart on page 58.

Critical Thinking

Put an X in the box next to the correct answer for questions 1, 3, and 4. Follow the directions provided for the other questions.

1. Which of the following statements from the article is an opinion rather than a fact?

☐ a. "Everything we do is music."

☐ b. Cage dropped out of college after two years.

☐ c. Until he died in 1992, Cage continued to enjoy listening to random sounds.

2. Choose from the letters below to correctly complete the following statement. Write the letters on the lines.

   In the article, _____ and _____ are alike because they both feature radios.

   a. Water Music

   b. Imaginary Landscape No. 4

   c. 4'33"

3. What was the effect of the performance of 4'33" at Maverick Concert Hall in 1952?

   ☐ a. Everyone in the audience loved the piece.

   ☐ b. Some people angrily left the concert hall.

   ☐ c. The audience demanded its money back.

4. Of the following theme categories, which would this story fit into?

   ☐ a. If it's not broken, don't fix it.

   ☐ b. Everything in its right place.

   ☐ c. If the shoe fits, wear it.

5. In which paragraph did you find your information or details to answer question 2?

   _____

   _____ Number of correct answers

   Record your personal assessment of your work on the Critical Thinking Chart on page 58.

Personal Response

What are you still curious about after finishing this article?

_____

_____

_____

_____

Self-Assessment

I really can't understand how

_____

_____

_____

_____

_____

_____

_____

_____

_____

_____

CRITICAL THINKING

Temple Grandin

Thinking in Pictures

Dr. Temple Grandin, who lives with autism, has challenged the cattle industry to treat cattle with more kindness.

Quick—what's your favorite animal? Is it a dog or a cat, or maybe a lion or a panda? You probably wouldn't say a cow. But Temple Grandin would, and she would be happy tell you all of the reasons why. Grandin makes no secret of the fact that she feels a special connection with cows because, as she says, she actually thinks like a cow. Through this unique ability to understand the minds of cows, Temple Grandin revolutionized the cattle industry.

2   Grandin was born in Massachusetts in 1947. By the time she was two, it was clear to her parents that she was not developing like other children. She didn't talk and she didn't like to be touched. She would engage in patterns of repetitive behaviors and sometimes fly into inexplicable rages. In short, Grandin demonstrated classic symptoms of autism, a complex brain disorder with no known cause or cure. Autism affects the areas of the brain that control language, complex thinking, and social interaction. That doesn't mean that all people with autism can't speak or can't cope in social situations. There are mild forms of autism and severe forms. For example, those who have weak social skills and who tend to focus on a narrow range of interests might have mild forms of autism.

Some people who might be considered eccentric—and this includes many scientists, inventors, and artists—may have mild forms of autism. People with severe forms of autism sometimes are completely nonverbal, unaware of their surroundings, or unable to control their behavior. When Temple Grandin was a child, doctors believed her angry outbursts and fear of other people put her in the category of severe autism. The doctors at that time believed that a person with such a condition could never lead a productive life. They thought she was so brain-damaged she should be placed in an institution for the rest of her life.

3   Luckily, Grandin's mother didn't listen to the doctors' advice. Instead, she sought out professionals to work one-on-one with her daughter. Thanks to full and careful therapy with a special caregiver, speech therapists, and private teachers, Grandin made great progress. She learned to talk, read, write, and bring her behavior under control. She was, as she later put it, "groping my way from the far side of darkness" toward the everyday world. By the time she was a teenager, Grandin was doing many of the things typical teens do, such as attending public school, performing science experiments, and building sets for the school play. However, she still struggled with certain areas of daily life. For example, Grandin was extremely sensitive to sound and touch. Anything that made a whirring noise sent her into a panic attack. She also had to endure ridicule from other kids at school who didn't understand her behavior and who labeled her "weird" and "nerdy."

4   When Grandin was 14, her mother sent her out West to spend time on a cattle ranch run by an aunt. Grandin watched with interest the ways in which the cattle reacted to their surroundings—the various sights, sounds, and smells. She observed that they disliked and feared being approached and took note of how they seemed to mistrust change. Grandin was amazed by how much these animals seemed to be like her. She realized that cattle rely on visual clues in order to make sense of their world, just as she did. She discovered that she and the animals were both "sensory thinkers" who

Grandin tests the reaction of cattle in a holding pen.

"think in pictures." Grandin's sense of identification with the animals grew so strong that she believed she could see and feel exactly what the animals saw and felt.

5   By 1970 Grandin had completed college and earned an advanced degree in animal science. She focused her studies on cattle behavior. As part of her research, Grandin visited a number of meat-packing plants. There she saw cattle being killed and their meat being prepared for sale. Grandin saw how the cattle were kept in holding pens and then moved into a chute for slaughter. The animals were put in restraining devices and held in place as a conveyor belt carried them through a chute. At the end of the chute, the animals were stunned into unconsciousness and then killed. It was clear to Grandin that the animals going into the chute were confused and also frightened. Some of them were so panic-stricken that they injured themselves trying to escape. Grandin felt that there was no need for the system to be so callous about the animals' feelings.

6   Grandin believed that a few simple changes would help to eliminate the stress and pain these animals were feeling. She saw, for example, that the meat-packing plants didn't have very good lighting at the entrance to the chute, and she could sense the animals' fear of being plunged into darkness. She saw that the slippery floor was causing the animals stress and that they were pushed and sometimes injured. Grandin designed a new kind of chute that included better lighting and a nonslip floor. She also published a list of 10 principles for the humane slaughter of livestock.

7   At first, only a few people in the meatpacking industry listened to Grandin. Plant owners were focused on making money, not on making animals comfortable. In the 1980s and 1990s, though, the public began to demand better treatment of livestock. Grandin showed that treating animals better actually led to increased profits for meat packers. Calm animals release fewer stress hormones into their bodies' systems, which translates into better quality meat. Calm animals also injure themselves less often, which means that less meat has to be thrown away because of bruises and other traumas. By 2010 more than half of all meatpacking plants in the United States had seen the wisdom of Grandin's message and had redesigned their plants accordingly.

8   Although Grandin has won many awards from animal-support organizations, she has always had her share of critics too. Some people believe that her work promotes the slaughter of animals. These critics argue that raising and killing livestock for food is unethical. They condemn Grandin for participating in the system. Grandin is aware of the criticisms. "I wish animals could have more than just a low-stress life and a quick, painless death," she says. "I wish animals could have a good life, too, with something useful to do." However, meatpacking plants are a reality, so she tries to make sure that animals that end up there at least get "a decent death."

9   As for her autism, Grandin says that in some ways it has been helpful to her. "My visual thinking gives me the ability to 'test-run' in my head a piece of equipment I've designed." Grandin acknowledges that people with severe autism labor under extreme limitations, but she also claims that "if you get a little bit of the trait, it's good." She can't understand scientists who want to get rid of all the genes that cause autism, because "then we'd be getting rid of a lot of talented and gifted people." Many would agree that Temple Grandin would certainly be counted among them. ✳

If you have been timed while reading this article, enter your reading time below. Then turn to the Words-per-Minute Table on page 55 and look up your reading speed (words per minute). Enter your reading speed on the graph on page 56.

Reading Time: Lesson 3

_____ : _____
Minutes   *Seconds*

A Finding the Main Idea

One statement below expresses the main idea of the article. One statement is too general, or too broad. The other statement explains only part of the article; it is too narrow. Label the statements using the following key:

M—Main Idea   **B—Too Broad**   **N—Too Narrow**

_____ 1. Sometimes what we might think of as a weakness turns out to be a benefit or a strength.

_____ 2. Temple Grandin's ability to think like cows allowed her to describe and suggest kinder ways to handle them, which led to more humane treatment of them.

_____ 3. Temple Grandin first became aware of her ability to think like cows when she visited a ranch that her aunt managed and immediately felt a connection to the cows there.

_____ Score 15 points for a correct M answer.

_____ Score 5 points for each correct B or N answer.

_____ **Total Score**: Finding the Main Idea

B Recalling Facts

How well do you remember the facts in the article? Put an X in the box next to the answer that correctly completes each statement about the article.

1. Autism is
   - ☐ a. a virus that is passed from person to person.
   - ☐ b. an easily curable disease.
   - ☐ c. a mysterious and complex brain disorder.

2. Grandin earned a degree in
   - ☐ a. psychology.
   - ☐ b. animal science.
   - ☐ c. mathematics.

3. Grandin said that cows feel fear when they
   - ☐ a. are moved into dark places.
   - ☐ b. are left alone.
   - ☐ c. see bright lights.

4. Meatpackers began to treat cattle better when
   - ☐ a. they felt sorry for the cattle they were about to slaughter.
   - ☐ b. the government told them they had to change.
   - ☐ c. they saw that they could make more money that way.

5. Some animal-support groups say that Grandin
   - ☐ a. does not understand how cows think.
   - ☐ b. is encouraging the slaughter of cattle.
   - ☐ c. is not realistic enough about how cattle must be killed.

Score 5 points for each correct answer.

_____ **Total Score**: Recalling Facts

C Making Inferences

When you combine your own experiences and information from a text to draw a conclusion that is not directly stated in that text, you are making an inference. Below are five statements that may or may not be inferences based on information in the article. Label the statements using the following key:

C—Correct Inference   **F—Faulty Inference**

_____ 1. Temple Grandin's mother probably spent a lot of money to fight Grandin's autism.

_____ 2. Meatpackers who do not follow Grandin's rules will not be able to stay in business.

_____ 3. Doctors cannot always predict accurately whether or not an autistic person will live a productive life.

_____ 4. Meatpackers eventually would have made up their own rules similar to Grandin's.

_____ 5. Grandin believes that people who are autistic have more to offer society than those who are not.

Score 5 points for each correct answer.

_____ **Total Score**: Making Inferences

D Using Words Precisely

Each numbered sentence below contains an underlined word or phrase from the article. Following the sentence are three definitions. One definition is closest to the meaning of the underlined word. One definition is opposite or nearly opposite. Label those two definitions using the following key. Do not label the remaining definition.

C—Closest   **O—Opposite or Nearly Opposite**

1. She would engage in patterns of repetitive behaviors and sometimes fly into <u>inexplicable</u> rages.

_____ a. hard to accept

_____ b. easy to understand

_____ c. impossible to explain

2. Some people who are considered <u>eccentric</u>—and this includes many scientists, inventors, and artists—may have mild forms of autism.

_____ a. normal, typical

_____ b. strange, peculiar

_____ c. witty, intelligent

3. Grandin felt that there was no need for the system to be so <u>callous</u> about the animals' feelings.

_____ a. cruel, insensitive

_____ b. moderate

_____ c. kindhearted

4. She also published a list of 10 principles for the <u>humane</u> slaughter of livestock.

_____ a. brutal and merciless

_____ b. fast and efficient

_____ c. considerate and kind

5. These critics argue that raising and killing livestock for food is <u>unethical</u>.

_____ a. without proper morals or honor

_____ b. honest, right

_____ c. puzzling

_____ Score 3 points for each correct C answer.

_____ Score 2 points for each correct O answer.

_____ **Total Score**: Using Words Precisely

Enter the four total scores in the spaces below, and add them together to find your Reading Comprehension Score. Then record your score on the graph on page 57.

Score	Question Type	Lesson 3
_____	Finding the Main Idea	
_____	Recalling Facts	
_____	Making Inferences	
_____	Using Words Precisely	
_____	**Reading Comprehension Score**	

Author's Approach

Put an X in the box next to the correct answer.

1. The author uses the first five sentences of the article to
   - ☐ a. introduce the reader to an unusual personality.
   - ☐ b. persuade the reader to prefer cows as a favorite animal.
   - ☐ c. entertain the reader with a game.

2. From the statements below, choose the one that you believe the author would agree with.
   - ☐ a. Grandin made her suggestions about animal treatment in order to become rich and famous.
   - ☐ b. Grandin truly cares about the well-being of cattle.
   - ☐ c. Grandin's belief that she thinks like cows is foolish and impossible to believe.

3. In this article, "Calm animals release fewer stress hormones into their bodies' systems, which translates into better quality meat" means
   - ☐ a. unless an animal is stress-free, its meat cannot be eaten.
   - ☐ b. meat that comes from calm animals does not taste as good as meat from stressed animals.
   - ☐ c. hormones released by stressed animals make their meat less desirable for eating.

4. What is the author's purpose in writing this article?
   - ☐ a. to encourage the reader to treat cattle better
   - ☐ b. to inform the reader about a unique, creative person
   - ☐ c. to express an opinion about whether people should slaughter cattle or not

---

_____ Number of correct answers

Record your personal assessment of your work on the Critical Thinking Chart on page 58.

CRITICAL THINKING

Summarizing and Paraphrasing

Follow the directions provided for question 1. Put an X in the box next to the correct answer for question 2.

1. Complete the following one-sentence summary of the article using the lettered phrases from the phrase bank below. Write the letters on the lines.

> **Phrase Bank:**
> a. Grandin's assertion that autism has helped her and should not be feared
> b. Grandin's suggestions for humane slaughter of livestock
> c. Grandin's early struggles with autism and her realization that she was similar to cows in many ways

The article, "Temple Grandin" begins with _____, goes on to describe _____, and ends with _____.

2. Read the statement from the article below. Then read the paraphrase of that statement. Choose the reason that best tells why the paraphrase does not say the same thing as the statement.

Statement: The animals were put in restraining devices and held in place as a conveyor belt carried them through a chute.

Paraphrase: After the animals fell down the chute, they had belts placed around them so they could not move.

☐ a. Paraphrase says too much.
☐ b. Paraphrase doesn't say enough.
☐ c. Paraphrase doesn't agree with the statement.

_____ Number of correct answers

Record your personal assessment of your work on the Critical Thinking Chart on page 58.

Critical Thinking

Follow the directions provided for questions 1 and 3. Put an X in the box next to the correct answer for questions 2 and 4.

1. For each statement below, write O if it expresses an opinion or write F if it expresses a fact.

_____ a. Meatpackers should be grateful to Temple Grandin for her suggestions for the humane slaughter of cattle.

_____ b. Temple Grandin first decided that she thought like cows when she visited her aunt on a ranch.

_____ c. In 2010 more than half of all meatpacking plants in the United States had redesigned their plants using Grandin's suggestions.

2. Using the information in paragraph 7, you can predict that

☐ a. consumers will decide that they no longer care whether cattle are afraid or uncomfortable.

☐ b. most meatpackers will soon go back to the way they slaughtered cattle before Grandin made her suggestions.

☐ c. even more meatpacking plants will take Grandin's suggestions for humane slaughtering.

3. Choose from the letters below to correctly complete the following statement. Write the letters on the lines.

According to the article, _____ caused doctors to _____, and the effect was _____.

a. recommend that Grandin be placed in an institution

b. Grandin's out-of-control behavior

c. Grandin's mother got her special help from professionals

CRITICAL THINKING

4. How is the article "Temple Grandin" an example of the theme of *Visionaries*?

☐ a. Temple Grandin suffered from autism but still managed to graduate from college.

☐ b. Temple Grandin had ideas that no one ever had before, and through her efforts, she made positive changes to society.

☐ c. Temple Grandin would be happy if all animals could live low-stress lives and decent deaths.

_____ Number of correct answers

Record your personal assessment of your work on the Critical Thinking Chart on page 58.

Personal Response

A question I would like Temple Grandin to answer is

_____

_____

_____

_____

Self-Assessment

The part I found most difficult about the article was

_____

_____

_____

_____

I found this difficult because

_____

_____

_____

_____

_____

_____

_____

_____

_____

_____

_____

CRITICAL THINKING

Who Turned on the Lights?

Tesla built a lightning laboratory, in which he created artificial lightning in flashes of millions of volts.

Almost everyone knows about Thomas Edison. The inventor of the light bulb and the phonograph is so much a part of American cultural history that we tend to accept him as the only outstanding contributor to modern electrical technology. Perhaps because of this, we have largely ignored the contributions of another visionary in the field, Nikola Tesla, who lived at the same time as Edison and who had many of the same goals. Who was Tesla? Some experts believe he was the greatest scientific genius of the modern era.

2   Before Tesla put pen to paper, he would work out the complete details of a new invention in his mind. He explained his creative process this way: "In my mind I change the construction, make improvements, and even operate the device. Without ever having drawn a sketch I can give the measurements of all parts to workmen, and when completed, all these parts will fit, just as certainly as though I had made the actual drawing." Tesla claimed that he didn't care if he ran the machine in his mind or in his shop. The results would be the same either way.

3   Tesla's inventions include a wide variety of electronic products, many of which still are in daily use. These include FM radio,

remote control devices, spark plugs, X-ray photographs, and both neon and fluorescent artificial lighting. Tesla's greatest achievement, however, was that he electrified the world.

4   Born in 1856, Tesla grew up in Croatia and immigrated to the United States in 1884. He arrived in New York City with only four cents in his pocket and a head full of ideas. He also carried a letter of recommendation to Thomas Edison from a scientist friend. This introduction won Tesla a job in Edison's laboratory. As it turned out, Tesla and Edison could not have been more different from each other in terms of culture, personality, and scientific point of view. Tesla was a sophisticated European who spoke eight languages. Edison was a down-to-earth, no-nonsense American. Edison was a careful, step-by-step inventor who wanted to create things people would use immediately. While Tesla did invent some practical things, he spent much of his time dreaming of fantastic new theories that might or might not work. One of the inventions he came up with turned out to be the cause of a major rivalry between the two men.

5   By the time Tesla came to work for him in 1884, Edison had already created the light bulb. He had also created the modern electric utility industry to provide the light bulb with a power source. By the end of the 1880s, cities across the country were putting up power stations every few miles to carry an electrical current called DC (for direct current). In a DC system, the electrical current flows in only one direction. Power

stations had to be close together because direct current could not travel more than two miles from the generator to the user before becoming too weak. Scientists at the time knew that direct current was inferior to alternating current (AC). In an AC system, the electrical current reverses direction at regular intervals. AC power could be sent over hundreds of miles with little power

loss. The problem with alternating current was that design flaws often caused its equipment to fail. Edison and the industry bosses were firmly behind the use of DC power, so direct current was the source of power for homes and factories.

6   Tesla, however, had figured out a more sure-fire system of transmitting AC electrical power. In Tesla's design, electric generators

"It seems I have always been ahead of my time," Tesla said near the end of his long career.

would send out energy in multiple waves that flowed in a repeating pattern, or cycle. He called this the *polyphase* principle. *Poly* means "more than one," and *phase* refers to a stage in the cycle. Alternating waves meant that power could be increased to very high-voltage levels, while the power loss across great distances could be kept at a minimum.

7   Tesla presented his idea to Edison, but Edison rejected it because he was not convinced that the high voltage that AC produced was safe. Edison was impressed with Tesla, though, so he offered Tesla a special project. He promised to pay $50,000 if Tesla could improve Edison's DC generator system. Tesla took up the challenge and worked for almost a year improving Edison's original DC design. When Tesla was finished Edison refused to pay him.

8   Embittered and angry, Tesla left the company and found himself right back where he started—penniless on the streets of New York City. He struggled to find whatever job he could. More and more, his thoughts returned to his AC design that he had presented to Edison. In his spare time Tesla put together the parts for the first working polyphase AC generator.

9   Tesla built the generator and also went on to produce AC-powered motors and transformers. In 1888 a successful businessman named George Westinghouse heard about Tesla and arranged to see a demonstration of his work. Westinghouse was amazed at the potential power of Tesla's AC-powered equipment. Westinghouse bought all of Tesla's patent rights, and the two became partners.

10   In 1892 Westinghouse won the contract to provide electricity to the huge World's Columbian Exposition in Chicago, which would open the following year. Edison had hoped to get the contract to use his DC power, but his price was much too high. Westinghouse won the contract by pledging to deliver more light than Edison could produce at half the price.

11   Tesla delivered on that promise and more. His AC power system lit up the Columbian exposition. In fact, he produced three times more energy than was being used by the rest of the city of Chicago! In addition, his AC generators powered the first-ever Ferris wheel and other rides and exhibits. Success tends to breed success, and Westinghouse and Tesla cashed in on the praise that was heaped upon them. Their national reputation ensured that they would be selected for more big projects.

12   In 1893 Westinghouse was awarded the contract to gather the massive energy of Niagara Falls to produce hydroelectric power. As usual, Tesla did not disappoint. The first power reached Buffalo, New York, at midnight, November 16, 1896. Within a few years, more generators at Niagara Falls were added. Power lines reached out in all directions. The Niagara Falls project meant the end of Edison's DC-generated power. Today, the entire world is lit by electricity sent by alternating current.

13   Tesla continued to develop new ideas for almost 50 years more, until his death in 1943. At the beginning of the 20th century, Tesla was performing significant research in such space-age fields as robotics, electric engines, and wireless communications. Some of the basic principles at the core of modern-day computer science were laid out by Tesla by as early as 1903.

14   One of history's overlooked inventors, Nikola Tesla had an uncommon ability to visualize the future in a way that few others could—or would even dare to try. ✳

If you have been timed while reading this article, enter your reading time below. Then turn to the Words-per-Minute Table on page 55 and look up your reading speed (words per minute). Enter your reading speed on the graph on page 56.

Reading Time: Lesson 4

_____ : _____
  Minutes   *Seconds*

A Finding the Main Idea

One statement below expresses the main idea of the article. One statement is too general, or too broad. The other statement explains only part of the article; it is too narrow. Label the statements using the following key:

M—Main Idea **B—Too Broad** **N—Too Narrow**

_____ 1. Nikola Tesla was a scientific genius and the inventor of the AC generator that electrified the world.

_____ 2. Nikola Tesla immigrated to the United States with only four cents in his pocket.

_____ 3. How the world is powered by electricity today is mainly the result of the work of one scientist, Nikola Tesla.

_____ Score 15 points for a correct M answer.

_____ Score 5 points for each correct B or N answer.

_____ **Total Score**: Finding the Main Idea

B Recalling Facts

How well do you remember the facts in the article? Put an X in the box next to the answer that correctly completes each statement about the article.

1. Nikola Tesla immigrated to the United States in
   ☐ a. 1856.
   ☐ b. 1884.
   ☐ c. 1892.

2. Thomas Edison invented
   ☐ a. the light bulb.
   ☐ b. FM radio.
   ☐ c. AC generators.

3. Edison rejected Tesla's idea for transmitting AC power because
   ☐ a. Tesla had not followed Edison's orders exactly.
   ☐ b. Edison was not convinced the high voltage was safe.
   ☐ c. Tesla's idea would never actually work.

4. In 1893 the World's Columbian Exposition was held in
   ☐ a. New York.
   ☐ b. Buffalo.
   ☐ c. Chicago.

5. The contract to harness the power of Niagara Falls was awarded to
   ☐ a. Thomas Edison.
   ☐ b. George Westinghouse.
   ☐ c. Nikola Tesla.

Score 5 points for each correct answer.

_____ **Total Score**: Recalling Facts

C Making Inferences

When you combine your own experiences and information from a text to draw a conclusion that is not directly stated in that text, you are making an inference. Below are five statements that may or may not be inferences based on information in the article. Label the statements using the following key:

C—Correct Inference   **F—Faulty Inference**

_____ 1. Nikola Tesla was extremely self-confident.

_____ 2. Light bulbs lit by AC are brighter than those lit by DC.

_____ 3. Like Edison, Westinghouse took unfair advantage of Tesla's work.

_____ 4. Because scientists agree that alternating current is better than direct current, it was only a matter of time before the switch was made from DC to AC.

_____ 5. The reason Tesla continued his research on the polyphase AC generator after he left Edison's company was to get back at Edison, his rival.

Score 5 points for each correct answer.

_____ **Total Score**: Making Inferences

D Using Words Precisely

Each numbered sentence below contains an underlined word or phrase from the article. Following the sentence are three definitions. One definition is closest to the meaning of the underlined word. One definition is opposite or nearly opposite. Label those two definitions using the following key. Do not label the remaining definition.

C—Closest   **O—Opposite or Nearly Opposite**

1. Tesla was a sophisticated European who spoke eight languages.

_____ a. wise in the ways of the world; cultured

_____ b. limited in experience of life

_____ c. secretive, not willing to express

2. Direct current is inferior to alternating current.

_____ a. better, finer

_____ b. similar, alike

_____ c. poor, worse in quality

3. In an AC system, the electrical current reverses direction at regular intervals.

_____ a. expected moments

_____ b. periods of time between two events

_____ c. continued event without breaks

4. Tesla was embittered when he left Edison's company.

_____ a. joyful

_____ b. anxious

_____ c. angered

5. Tesla continued to perform <u>significant</u> research in a number of fields.

_____ a. meaningful, worthwhile

_____ b. astonishing, surprising

_____ c. small, minor

_____ Score 3 points for each correct C answer.

_____ Score 2 points for each correct O answer.

_____ **Total Score**: Using Words Precisely

Enter the four total scores in the spaces below, and add them together to find your Reading Comprehension Score. Then record your score on the graph on page 57.

Score	Question Type	Lesson 4
_____	Finding the Main Idea	
_____	Recalling Facts	
_____	Making Inferences	
_____	Using Words Precisely	
_____	**Reading Comprehension Score**	

Author's Approach

Put an X in the box next to the correct answer.

1. What is the author's purpose in writing this article?

☐ a. to encourage the reader to study science

☐ b. to inform the reader about the work of Nikola Tesla

☐ c. to describe two systems of sending and receiving electrical power

2. From the statements below, choose the ones that you believe the author would agree with.

☐ a. Edison had very good reason not to pay the $50,000 he had promised to Tesla.

☐ b. Westinghouse was a very clever businessman to see the value of Tesla's inventions.

☐ c. Tesla deserves more credit for his invention of the system that lit the world.

3. Judging by statements from the article "Who Turned on the Lights?" you can conclude that the author wants the reader to think that

☐ a. Tesla should be as famous as Edison is now.

☐ b. all of Tesla's solutions to scientific problems were better than Edison's.

☐ c. there have not been any first-rate American inventors since the 1800s.

_____ Number of correct answers

Record your personal assessment of your work on the Critical Thinking Chart on page 58.

CRITICAL THINKING

Summarizing and Paraphrasing

Put an X in the box next to the correct answer for questions 1 and 2. Follow the directions provided for question 3.

1. Choose the best one-sentence paraphrase for the following sentence from the article: "Edison was a down-to-earth, no-nonsense American."

☐ a.   Edison was a sensible, practical American who would not put up with foolishness.

☐ b.   Edison was a humble American, but he had no sense of humor.

☐ c.   Edison was an American who was stubborn and difficult to work with.

2. Choose the sentence that correctly restates the following sentence from the article: "Tesla arrived in New York City with only four cents in his pocket and a head full of ideas."

☐ a.   On arrival, Tesla kept four cents and his ideas in his pocket.

☐ b.   Tesla had nothing of any value when he arrived.

☐ c.   When Tesla arrived, he had plenty of ideas but hardly any money.

3. Reread paragraph 4 in the article. Below, write a summary of the paragraph in no more than 15 words.

_____

_____

_____

_____

_____

_____

_____ Number of correct answers

Record your personal assessment of your work on the Critical Thinking Chart on page 58.

CRITICAL THINKING

Critical Thinking

Put an X in the box next to the correct answer for questions 1, 4, and 5. Follow the directions provided for the other questions.

1. From the article, you can predict that if Tesla were successful today, he would be

☐ a.   coming up with new ideas and inventing things.

☐ b.   trying to win popular approval for his past ideas.

☐ c.   trying to make a better light bulb.

2. Choose from the letters below to correctly complete the following statement. Write the letters on the lines.

In the article, _____ and _____ are alike because they were both inventors.

a.   Edison

b.   Tesla

c.   Westinghouse

3. Reread paragraph 12. Then choose from the letters below to correctly complete the following statement. Write the letters on the lines.

According to paragraph 12, _____ because _____.

a.   Tesla's AC-powered Niagara Falls project was successful

b.   Edison's DC-generated power was no longer used

c.   Westinghouse was awarded the contract to gather and deliver the energy of Niagara Falls

4. How is "Who Turned on the Lights?" an example of the theme of *Visionaries*?

☐ a.   The late 1800s were a time of great change.

☐ b.   Tesla and Edison did not agree on the method of transmitting electrical power.

☐ c.   Tesla could envision new solutions to problems and took action toward making his ideas become reality.

5. What did you have to do to answer question 2?

☐ a. find a comparison (how things are the same)

☐ b. find a fact (something that you can prove is true)

☐ c. find a contrast (how things are different)

_____ Number of correct answers

Record your personal assessment of your work on the Critical Thinking Chart on page 58.

Personal Response

The most interesting thing about Nikola Tesla is

_____

_____

_____

_____

_____

_____

Self-Assessment

Which concepts or ideas from the article were difficult to understand?

_____

_____

_____

_____

_____

Which were easy to understand?

_____

_____

_____

_____

_____

_____

CRITICAL THINKING

The Bullet Stopper

Police Commissioner Raymond Kelly shows where the bullet fired from a .38 caliber gun struck a bulletproof vest worn by Officer Robert Salerno.

On March 22, 2010, New York City Police Officer Robert Salerno was shot three times in the line of duty, twice in the lower abdomen and once in the chest. The bullets to the abdomen required emergency surgery. The one to the chest would have been fatal if Salerno hadn't been wearing a bulletproof vest. "Officer Salerno, a brave young man, is very lucky," said Police Commissioner Raymond Kelly shortly after the incident. "It could have been much worse." Officer Salerno is certainly not the only officer who should be counting lucky stars. While *bulletproof* does not mean "foolproof"—bulletproof vests protect only the upper body and are vulnerable to high-powered rifle bullets—these vests have saved the lives of thousands of police officers. For that, these officers can thank a chemist named Stephanie Kwolek. She is the one who invented Kevlar, the material used to make the lifesaving vests.

2   Kwolek didn't intend to be a chemist. Growing up in Pennsylvania during the 1920s and 1930s, she thought she was going to become a doctor. It was her father who sparked her early interest in science. "I remember trudging through the woods near my house with him and looking for snakes and other animals," she told one reporter. "We also studied the various wild plants and leaves and seeds." At Margaret Morrison Carnegie College (now Carnegie Mellon University), she majored in chemistry. She took lots of other science courses as well because she knew she would need them to get into medical school. After Kwolek graduated, however, she realized she didn't have enough money to attend medical school right away. With her chemistry background, she was able to get a job as a researcher with the DuPont Corporation, a leading chemical company.

3   Kwolek arrived at DuPont just eight years after the company pioneered and developed nylon, the first synthetic fiber. She began exploring other new polymer fibers and ways to make them. A polymer is large molecule composed of a network of many repeating units. It is formed by chemically bonding together identical or similar smaller molecules called monomers. In Greek, *poly* means "many" and *mono* means "one." Basically her job was to experiment with a variety of polymers to see if any of them would make an interesting new fiber. As it turned out, she loved this job. "I became so interested in the research I was doing at DuPont, solving problems and constantly learning, that I changed my mind and did not go to medical school." Instead she devoted her life to chemistry and polymer science.

Stephanie Kwolek discovered a synthetic fiber that is five times stronger than steel.

4   In 1964 Kwolek's research group decided to look for a new high-performance lightweight fiber that could be used in automobile tires to increase gas mileage. Lighter, stiffer tires would roll easier. The smoother ride would reduce the amount of gasoline used. "A number of people had been asked to take up this project, and no one seemed to be interested," said Kwolek. "So I was asked if I would do it."

5   Call it a lucky break, but in the course of this work Kwolek discovered a polymer that displayed many strange features. It formed liquid crystals in a solution. This was something no other polymer had ever done. Up to this point, all polymer molecules had bends that made them look like spaghetti. These polymer molecules, however, were perfectly straight, like match sticks. Also, the polymer solution looked cloudy rather than clear, like the way other polymer solutions looked. "I think someone who wasn't thinking very much or just wasn't aware or took less interest in it would have thrown it out," Kwolek said. Luckily, Kwolek's ability to investigate something that she didn't expect prevented her from doing that. As she once remarked, "If things don't work out, I don't just throw them out, I struggle over them to try and see if there's something there."

6   This particularly weird polymer intrigued and perplexed Kwolek. She wanted to "spin" it in a machine called a spinneret. This would filter the polymers down into long, thin strands. At first, the laboratory technician refused to spin the new mysterious polymer, claiming it wouldn't spin and would clog his machine's tiny holes. He figured a polymer solution this cloudy surely had some solid particles in it. Kwolek patiently insisted until at last he agreed to spin it. "I think either I wore him down or else he felt sorry for me," Kwolek later recalled. The polymer didn't clog the spinneret. When the new fiber came out, it was at least nine times stiffer than anything she had ever created before. As much as Kwolek wanted to believe these amazing results, she didn't really trust them. She sent the polymers back several times for retesting, but the results were always the same. After a great deal more work and further experiments, DuPont announced in 1971 its new fiber called Kevlar. This heat-resistant material was five times stronger than steel, yet it was incredibly light.

7   Over the years, scientists have been able to find more than 200 useful applications for Kevlar. With its unique combination of toughness and heat stability, Kevlar is now used in such products as automobile brake pads, tires, protective gloves, and fiber optic cables. It is used in space vehicles, skis, parachutes, and boats, but police officers such as Robert Salerno are especially thankful that Kevlar is used in bulletproof vests as well. How can something so light and flexible stop a speeding bullet? Multiple layers of Kevlar fibers form a "web" that absorbs and disperses the impact energy of the bullet. Because the fibers work together both in the individual layer and with other layers of material in the vest, they are able to dissipate the force of the bullet and prevent it from penetrating the body.

8   Kevlar-lined bulletproof vests have saved untold lives in the 40-plus years they have been on the market. One thankful Virginia police officer even had Kwolek autograph his vest after it stopped a bullet. That officer's vest literally has Kwolek's name on it, but in another sense, all of the vests do. ✳

If you have been timed while reading this article, enter your reading time below. Then turn to the Words-per-Minute Table on page 55 and look up your reading speed (words per minute). Enter your reading speed on the graph on page 56.

Reading Time: Lesson 5

_____ : _____
Minutes   *Seconds*

A Finding the Main Idea

One statement below expresses the main idea of the article. One statement is too general, or too broad. The other statement explains only part of the article; it is too narrow. Label the statements using the following key:

M—Main Idea   **B—Too Broad**   **N—Too Narrow**

_____ 1. Kevlar, invented by Stephanie Kwolek, is used in bulletproof vests that protect wearers from injury caused by speeding bullets.

_____ 2. Chemist Stephanie Kwolek is credited with inventing Kevlar, a tough, stable material now used in many products.

_____ 3. Research and experiments involving polymers have yielded some useful products.

_____ Score 15 points for a correct M answer.

_____ Score 5 points for each correct B or N answer.

_____ **Total Score**: Finding the Main Idea

B Recalling Facts

How well do you remember the facts in the article? Put an X in the box next to the answer that correctly completes each statement about the article.

1. Before she got a job as a researcher, Stephanie Kwolek had planned to become a
    ☐ a. doctor.
    ☐ b. dentist.
    ☐ c. lawyer.

2. Before she discovered Kevlar, Kwolek had been looking for
    ☐ a. a lightweight fiber for car tires.
    ☐ b. material that could be used in bulletproof vests.
    ☐ c. a lightweight material for parachutes.

3. The polymer molecules Kwolek found were
    ☐ a. curved, like spaghetti.
    ☐ b. zig-zag-shaped, like lightning.
    ☐ c. straight, like match sticks.

4. A spinneret is designed to
    ☐ a. change the color of polymers.
    ☐ b. combine various polymers to make new ones.
    ☐ c. filter polymers into long, thin strands.

5. DuPont announced Kevlar to the public in
    ☐ a. 1952.
    ☐ b. 1971.
    ☐ c. 1994.

Score 5 points for each correct answer.

_____ **Total Score**: Recalling Facts

C Making Inferences

When you combine your own experiences and information from a text to draw a conclusion that is not directly stated in that text, you are making an inference. Below are five statements that may or may not be inferences based on information in the article. Label the statements using the following key:

C—Correct Inference   **F—Faulty Inference**

_____ 1. Kwolek's father was a scientist who pushed his daughter to study biology.

_____ 2. The success of the DuPont Corporation depends mostly on the work of its researchers.

_____ 3. Kwolek trusted her own research abilities and those of her co-workers so much that she never had to repeat tests.

_____ 4. The spinneret that was used to test Kwolek's polymer molecules was a sensitive and expensive machine.

_____ 5. Probably all of the possible uses of Kevlar have already been found.

Score 5 points for each correct answer.

_____ **Total Score**: Making Inferences

D Using Words Precisely

Each numbered sentence below contains an underlined word or phrase from the article. Following the sentence are three definitions. One definition is closest to the meaning of the underlined word. One definition is opposite or nearly opposite. Label those two definitions using the following key. Do not label the remaining definition.

C—Closest   **O—Opposite or Nearly Opposite**

1. Kwolek arrived at DuPont just eight years after the company pioneered the creation of nylon, the first <u>synthetic</u> fiber.

   _____ a. wrinkle-proof

   _____ b. artificial

   _____ c. naturally occurring

2. This particularly weird polymer <u>intrigued</u> and perplexed Kwolek.

   _____ a. bored

   _____ b. made curious

   _____ c. caused trouble

3. With its unique combination of toughness and heat <u>stability</u>, Kevlar is now used in a number of everyday products.

   _____ a. resistance to change

   _____ b. great chance of breaking down

   _____ c. appeal

4. Multiple layers of Kevlar fibers form a "web" that absorbs and <u>disperses</u> the impact energy of the bullet.

   _____ a. focuses in one place

   _____ b. interferes with

   _____ c. scatters

5. Because the fibers work together, both in the individual layer and with other layers of material in the vest, they are able to <u>dissipate</u>, the force of the bullet.

_____ a. change

_____ b. make stronger

_____ c. reduce or cause to vanish

_____ Score 3 points for each correct C answer.

_____ Score 2 points for each correct O answer.

_____ **Total Score**: Using Words Precisely

Enter the four total scores in the spaces below, and add them together to find your Reading Comprehension Score. Then record your score on the graph on page 57.

Score	Question Type	Lesson 5
_____	Finding the Main Idea	
_____	Recalling Facts	
_____	Making Inferences	
_____	Using Words Precisely	
_____	**Reading Comprehension Score**	

Author's Approach

Put an X in the box next to the correct answer.

1. The main purpose of the first paragraph is to
   - ☐ a. describe one important use of Kevlar and identify its inventor.
   - ☐ b. explain how Kevlar works.
   - ☐ c. make the reader feel sorry for and grateful to Officer Robert Salerno.

2. What is the author's purpose in writing this article?
   - ☐ a. to encourage the reader to become a scientific researcher
   - ☐ b. to inform the reader about an inventor whose curiosity and intelligence led to an important discovery
   - ☐ c. to describe what happens when a speeding bullet hits a Kevlar vest

3. Which of the following statements from the article best describes the way Kwolek did her research?
   - ☐ a. "A number of people had been asked to take up this project, and no one seemed to be interested."
   - ☐ b. "If things don't work out, I don't just throw them out, I struggle over them to try and see if there's something there."
   - ☐ c. "I think either I wore him down or else he felt sorry for me."

_____ Number of correct answers

Record your personal assessment of your work on the Critical Thinking Chart on page 58.

Summarizing and Paraphrasing

Follow the directions provided for question 1. Put an X in the box next to the correct answer for question 2.

1. Read the statement from the article below. Then read the paraphrase of that statement. Choose the reason that best tells why the paraphrase does not say the same thing as the statement.

   Statement: This heat-resistant material was five times stronger than steel, yet it was incredibly light.

   Paraphrase: Although the material was heat resistant and lighter than steel, steel was five times stronger than the material.

   ☐ a. Paraphrase says too much.

   ☐ b. Paraphrase doesn't say enough.

   ☐ c. Paraphrase doesn't agree with the statement.

2. Below are summaries of the article. Choose the summary that says all the most important things about the article but in the fewest words.

   ☐ a. Kevlar is a lightweight, strong material that is used in many products, such as bulletproof vests, auto tires, and parachutes.

   ☐ b. Stephanie Kwolek, a researcher at DuPont Corporation, experimented with polymers and eventually invented Kevlar, a strong material with many uses.

   ☐ c. Chemist Stephanie Kwolek had been working with polymer molecules when she found one that was different from others she was familiar with. So she had it spun in a spinneret several times and finally concluded that its fibers were amazingly strong and lightweight.

   _____ Number of correct answers

   Record your personal assessment of your work on the Critical Thinking Chart on page 58.

Critical Thinking

Follow the directions provided for questions 1 and 2. Put an X next to the correct answer for the other questions.

1. For each statement below, write O if it expresses an opinion or write F if it expresses a fact.

   _____ a. Stephanie Kwolek was probably the finest chemist on the DuPont staff.

   _____ b. The laboratory technician should not have refused to spin Kwolek's unusual polymer so many times.

   _____ c. Scientists have found hundreds of uses for Kevlar.

2. Choose from the letters below to correctly complete the following statement. Write the letters on the lines.

   According to the article, _____ causes them to _____, and the effect is _____.

   a. less gasoline is used to keep cars moving

   b. roll more easily

   c. making auto tires from lighter, stiffer materials

3. If you were a beginning research scientist, how could you use the information in the article to help you make discoveries?

   ☐ a. Pay attention to unusual findings and follow where they lead.

   ☐ b. Like Kwolek, you must first have a childhood interest in science.

   ☐ c. Don't spend a lot of time on ideas that have not been proven.

4. What did you have to do to answer question 3?

☐ a. find a comparison (how things are the same)

☐ b. find a fact (something that you can prove is true)

☐ c. draw a conclusion (a sensible statement based on the text and your experience)

_____ Number of correct answers

Record your personal assessment of your work on the Critical Thinking Chart on page 58.

Personal Response

A question I would like answered by Stephanie Kwolek is

_____

_____

_____

_____

_____

_____

_____

Self-Assessment

Before reading this article, I already knew

_____

_____

_____

_____

_____

_____

_____

_____

_____

_____

_____

_____

_____

_____

Compare and Contrast

Think about the articles you have read in Unit One. Choose three articles that were the most complicated or confusing. Write the titles of the articles in the first column of the chart below. Use information you learned from the articles to fill in the empty boxes in the chart.

Title	What idea or process does the article discuss?	Which parts of the article were confusing to you?	Which parts of the article made the most sense?

Imagine that you could speak to one of the visionaries in the articles. What part of the article would you ask them to explain?_____

_____

_____

_____ .

Words-per-Minute Table

Unit One

Directions If you were timed while reading an article, refer to the Reading Time you recorded in the box at the end of the article. Use this words-per-minute table to determine your reading speed for that article. Then plot your reading speed on the graph on page 56.

Lesson	Sample	1	2	3	4	5	
No. of Words	1135	1145	1090	1189	1163	1017	
1:30	757	763	727	793	775	678	90
1:40	681	687	654	713	698	610	100
1:50	619	625	595	649	634	555	110
2:00	568	573	545	595	582	509	120
2:10	524	528	503	549	537	469	130
2:20	486	491	467	510	498	436	140
2:30	454	458	436	476	465	407	150
2:40	426	429	409	446	436	381	160
2:50	401	404	385	420	410	359	170
3:00	378	382	363	396	388	339	180
3:10	358	362	344	375	367	321	190
3:20	341	344	327	357	349	305	200
3:30	324	327	311	340	332	291	210
3:40	310	312	297	324	317	277	220
3:50	296	299	284	310	303	265	230
4:00	284	286	273	297	291	254	240
4:10	272	275	262	285	279	244	250
4:20	262	264	252	274	268	235	260
4:30	252	254	242	264	258	226	270
4:40	243	245	234	255	249	218	280
4:50	235	237	226	246	241	210	290
5:00	227	229	218	238	233	203	300
5:10	220	222	211	230	225	197	310
5:20	213	215	204	223	218	191	320
5:30	206	208	198	216	211	185	330
5:40	200	202	192	210	205	179	340
5:50	195	196	187	204	199	174	350
6:00	189	191	182	198	194	170	360
6:10	184	186	177	193	189	165	370
6:20	179	181	172	188	184	161	380
6:30	175	176	168	183	179	156	390
6:40	170	172	164	178	174	153	400
6:50	166	168	160	174	170	149	410
7:00	162	164	156	170	166	145	420
7:10	158	160	152	166	162	142	430
7:20	155	156	149	162	159	139	440
7:30	151	153	145	159	155	136	450
7:40	148	149	142	155	152	133	460
7:50	145	146	139	152	148	130	470
8:00	142	143	136	149	145	127	480

Minutes and Seconds

Seconds

Plotting Your Progress: Reading Speed

Unit One

Directions If you were timed while reading an article, write your words-per-minute rate for that article in the box under the number of the lesson. Then plot your reading speed on the graph by putting a small X on the line directly above the number of the lesson, across from the number of words per minute you read. As you mark your speed for each lesson, graph your progress by drawing a line to connect the Xs.

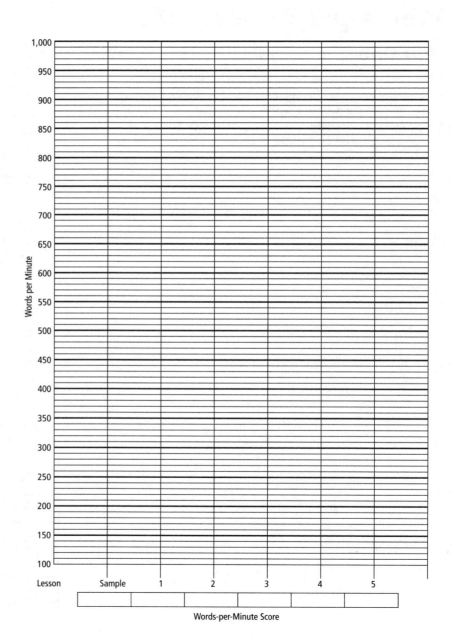

Plotting Your Progress: Reading Comprehension

Unit One

Directions Write your Reading Comprehension score for each lesson in the box under the number of the lesson. Then plot your score on the graph by putting a small X on the line directly above the number of the lesson and across from the score you earned. As you mark your score for each lesson, graph your progress by drawing a line to connect the Xs.

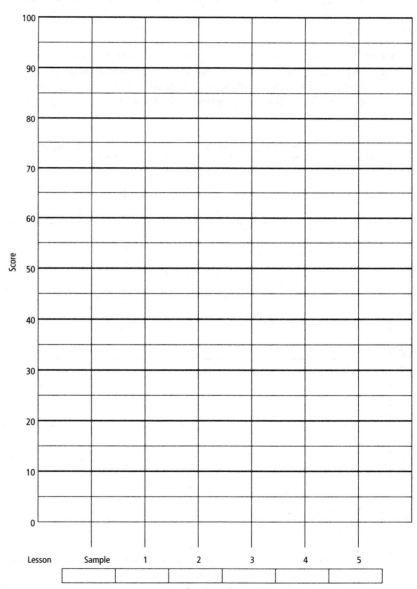

Score

Lesson   Sample   1   2   3   4   5

Reading Comprehension Score

Plotting Your Progress: Critical Thinking

Unit One

Directions Work with your teacher to evaluate your responses to the Critical Thinking questions for each lesson. Then fill in the appropriate spaces in the chart below. For each lesson and each type of Critical Thinking question, do the following: Mark a minus sign (–) in the box to indicate areas in which you feel you could improve. Mark a plus sign (+) to indicate areas in which you feel you did well. Mark a minus-slash-plus sign (–/+) to indicate areas in which you had mixed success. Then write any comments you have about your performance, including ideas for improvement.

Lesson	Author's Approach	Summarizing and Paraphrasing	Critical Thinking
Sample			
1			
2			
3			
4			
5			

Unit Two

Whatever It Takes

Maurice Wilson set off on his daring adventure to Mount Everest just one month after this first-ever flight over the peak.

He was so incredibly resolute in his purpose, and so confident in his ability to carry it out, that his followers and critics called him "the Madman of Everest." Eight years earlier, in 1924, British mountaineers George Mallory and Andrew Irvine had died attempting to climb to the top of Mount Everest, the world's highest mountain. Now here was another British man who had decided to try a new, truly original strategy to reach the mountain's summit. Maurice Wilson declared that he would fly a plane to Mount Everest, purposely crash-land high up on the slopes, and then walk to the summit. Critics pointed to two rather significant details that could stand in Wilson's way of achieving this goal. First of all, Wilson had never flown an airplane before or even been inside one. Secondly, Wilson had never before climbed a mountain. But Wilson believed that he could do anything he set his mind to if he applied the right amount of willpower, faith, and discipline.

2   Wilson had joined the British army on his 18th birthday to fight in World War I. He was a courageous soldier, and he rose swiftly through the ranks to become a captain. Wilson was injured by machine gun fire and later released from duty. His war wounds never fully healed, and his left arm in particular bothered him for the rest of his life. Wilson found the transition back to civilian life difficult. He drifted from here to there, living in England, the United States, and New Zealand. Although he made money in a variety of businesses, Wilson could find no satisfaction.

3   Then his life rather mysteriously changed direction. On a boat journey from New Zealand to England, Wilson met some Indian mystics known as yogis. Wilson was fascinated by what they told him about the incredible powers of meditation and fasting. So when Wilson came down with tuberculosis later that year, he decided to use the yogis' approach to cure himself of this deadly lung disease. Rather than seeing a doctor, Wilson undertook a rigorous program of fasting, prayer, and long walks. Because the routine apparently worked—his health returned—Wilson became convinced that he could do anything. To prove it, he decided to do something truly amazing. For him, that meant conquering Mount Everest all by himself. Everyone told him his idea was impossible, but their doubts only served to fuel his raging determination.

4   Wilson began hiking in local hills to get his legs in shape for the trek. He bought a used Gipsy Moth biplane and began taking flying lessons. He was a mediocre student; his instructor commented that Wilson had learned how to fly, but he lacked the instincts to be a really good pilot. On one of Wilson's first solo flights, he hit a hedge during his landing and flipped his plane, leaving him hanging upside down in the cockpit.

5   After getting his plane repaired, Wilson left London on May 21, 1933, to fly the 5,000 miles to the Himalaya mountain range, on the border of Nepal and Tibet. From there he would begin to ascend to the top of Mount Everest. Airplanes at this time were still not very common. Airports were very scarce, runways were unpaved, and there was no radar or tracking equipment. All Wilson had to guide him were some simple maps. No one gave him better than a one-in-a-million chance of arriving there safely.

Wilson rested here, at the Rongbuk Monastery in Tibet, before setting out on the final leg of his journey.

6   Not only did Wilson have no support or experience, he also got in trouble with his own government. They sent him a telegram instructing him not to begin the journey until he got permission to climb Everest from the government of Nepal. Wilson tore up the telegram and continued with his plans. He had expected to fly over Persia (now Iran), but when that government refused him permission to use their airspace, he was forced take a longer route. Once in the air, he followed the coast down the Persian Gulf, sticking his head out the side of his open cockpit to see where he was going. The British government tried to stop him by asking airports not to give him any fuel. Somehow, though, Wilson bluffed or lied his way into getting the fuel he needed. It took him two full weeks, but he finally made it to India. Given his lack of flying experience, the detours, and pressure from the government, his 6,000-mile flight was a stunning achievement. He should have quit while he was ahead.

7   India did not welcome Wilson with open arms. In fact, the Indian authorities immediately seized his plane until they had completed their investigation of his plans. Three weeks later Wilson got his airplane back, but by then the monsoon season had begun. Even he had to admit that it would be too dangerous to fly to Mount Everest through heavy rains and storms. Because he was running out of money, Wilson sold his plane and forced himself to stop and spend the winter in Darjeeling, India. Then came another setback. Indian authorities denied him permission to enter the Himalayas— even on foot. If he wanted to climb Mount Everest, he would have to travel to the mountain undetected.

8   On March 21, 1934, Wilson disguised himself as a Tibetan monk and slipped out of Darjeeling before dawn, accompanied by three hired local guides called Sherpas. Traveling swiftly at night, the foursome covered 300 miles, first through jungles and then up into the mountains. After just 25 days, they reached Wilson's first objective— the Rongbuk Monastery, 16,500 feet high on the slopes of Mount Everest. Wilson prayed and fasted here for two days, then he set out alone to conquer the peak. He managed to climb to 17,600 feet, but he found himself facing huge cliffs of ice that he didn't know how to climb, as well as a furious blizzard. He retreated back to the monastery with his face half-paralyzed from the cold and his war-wounded left arm hanging limp.

9   A month later, Wilson tried again. He paid two Sherpas to lead him to 21,000 feet and told them to wait there while he climbed to the summit. Again, without the proper equipment, he struggled to get his footing on the icy glaciers. After three futile days he was forced to climb down to the waiting Sherpas. For any ordinary person, that probably would have been enough, but Maurice Wilson was no ordinary person. He was grimly determined to reach the summit of Mount Everest. The Sherpas were shocked when, a few days later, Wilson announced his intention to make a third attempt. This time the Sherpas refused to help. Seeing how physically battered he was, they implored him to give up.

10   On May 29, 1934, Wilson set out again to scale the highest peak on Earth. After resting for a day at 21,500 feet, he pushed on toward the top. The final entry in his diary brightly states, "Off again. Gorgeous day." Wilson's body was found a year later by mountaineers on their way to the summit. The best guess is that he died from exposure to the cold and exhaustion. He was just 7500 feet from completing his dream—an extraordinary achievement for quite an extraordinary man. ✷

If you have been timed while reading this article, enter your reading time below. Then turn to the Words-per-Minute Table on page 101 and look up your reading speed (words per minute). Enter your reading speed on the graph on page 102.

Reading Time: Lesson 6

_____ : _____

Minutes   *Seconds*

A Finding the Main Idea

One statement below expresses the main idea of the article. One statement is too general, or too broad. The other statement explains only part of the article; it is too narrow. Label the statements using the following key:

M—Main Idea   **B—Too Broad**   **N—Too Narrow**

_____ 1. Maurice Wilson was a truly original person.

_____ 2. Maurice Wilson left England to climb Mount Everest in 1933.

_____ 3. Maurice Wilson was a man who thought he could do anything, even reach the top of Mount Everest.

_____ Score 15 points for a correct M answer.

_____ Score 5 points for each correct B or N answer.

_____ **Total Score**: Finding the Main Idea

B Recalling Facts

How well do you remember the facts in the article? Put an X in the box next to the answer that correctly completes each statement about the article.

1. Maurice Wilson joined the army to fight in
   ☐ a. the Civil War.
   ☐ b. World War I.
   ☐ c. World War II.

2. After the war, Wilson lived in England, the United States, and
   ☐ a. Australia.
   ☐ b. Tibet.
   ☐ c. New Zealand.

3. Persia is now called
   ☐ a. Iraq.
   ☐ b. Iran.
   ☐ c. India.

4. In March 1934 Wilson left Darjeeling, India, disguised as a
   ☐ a. Tibetan monk.
   ☐ b. Sherpa guide.
   ☐ c. Indian official.

5. After his first attempt, Wilson rested at the Rongbuk Monastery for
   ☐ a. one month.
   ☐ b. one year.
   ☐ c. three months.

Score 5 points for each correct answer.

_____ **Total Score**: Recalling Facts

C Making Inferences

When you combine your own experiences and information from a text to draw a conclusion that is not directly stated in that text, you are making an inference. Below are five statements that may or may not be inferences based on information in the article. Label the statements using the following key:

C—Correct Inference   **F—Faulty Inference**

_____ 1. Officials tried to stop Wilson from climbing Mount Everest because they were concerned for his safety.

_____ 2. Wilson did not have a clear idea of how cold and icy Mount Everest could be.

_____ 3. If Wilson had survived his third attempt, he would have taken the Sherpas' advice and quit.

_____ 4. In 1934 not many people had attempted to climb Mount Everest.

_____ 5. Wilson was worried about what the British government would do to him if he succeeded.

Score 5 points for each correct answer.

_____ **Total Score**: Making Inferences

D Using Words Precisely

Each numbered sentence below contains an underlined word or phrase from the article. Following the sentence are three definitions. One definition is closest to the meaning of the underlined word. One definition is opposite or nearly opposite. Label those two definitions using the following key. Do not label the remaining definition.

C—Closest   **O—Opposite or Nearly Opposite**

1. Wilson was <u>resolute</u> in his purpose.

_____ a. undecided

_____ b. wise

_____ c. determined, single-minded

2. Wilson undertook a <u>rigorous</u> program of fasting, prayer, and long walks.

_____ a. adventurous

_____ b. severe, strict

_____ c. easy-going, mild

3. His flying instructor said that Wilson was a <u>mediocre</u> student.

_____ a. thoughtless, inconsiderate

_____ b. exceptional, superior

_____ c. average, ordinary

4. Because authorities denied him permission to enter the Himalayas, Wilson would have to travel to the mountain <u>undetected</u>.

_____ a. unnoticed

_____ b. visible

_____ c. unprepared

5. After three <u>futile</u> days, Wilson was forced to climb down to the waiting Sherpas.

_____ a. difficult, challenging

_____ b. unsuccessful, useless

_____ c. hopeful, productive

_____ Score 3 points for each correct C answer.

_____ Score 2 points for each correct O answer.

_____ **Total Score**: Using Words Precisely

Enter the four total scores in the spaces below, and add them together to find your Reading Comprehension Score. Then record your score on the graph on page 103.

Score	Question Type	Lesson 6
_____	Finding the Main Idea	
_____	Recalling Facts	
_____	Making Inferences	
_____	Using Words Precisely	
_____	**Reading Comprehension Score**	

Author's Approach

Put an X in the box next to the correct answer.

1. From the statements below, choose the one that you believe the author would agree with.

☐ a. Maurice Wilson didn't care about society's disapproval of his plans or his behavior.

☐ b. Wilson's plan of crashing a plane into Mount Everest and then climbing alone to the top was a brilliant plan.

☐ c. You do not need to learn any mountaineering skills to climb Mount Everest.

2. In this article, "Wilson found the transition back to civilian life difficult" means

☐ a. after the war, civilians made life difficult for Wilson.

☐ b. Wilson had a hard time going back to being a civilian.

☐ c. Wilson thought the life of a soldier was easier than the life of a civilian.

3. Which of these statements best describes Wilson?

☐ a. Maurice Wilson lacked the instincts to be a really good pilot.

☐ b. Wilson was not an ordinary person.

☐ c. Wilson believed that he could do anything he set his mind to if he applied the right amount of willpower, faith, and discipline.

_____ Number of correct answers

Record your personal assessment of your work on the Critical Thinking Chart on page 104.

CRITICAL THINKING

Summarizing and Paraphrasing

Put an X in the box next to the correct answer for question 1. Follow the directions provided for the other questions.

1. Choose the best one-sentence paraphrase for the following sentence from the article: "India did not welcome Wilson with open arms."

   ☐ a. No one in India hugged Wilson when he arrived.

   ☐ b. India did not pay any attention to Wilson.

   ☐ c. India was not very pleased with Wilson and his plans.

2. Complete the following one-sentence summary of the article using the lettered phrases from the phrase bank below. Write the letters on the lines.

   > **Phrase Bank:**
   > a. Wilson's journey to India
   > b. Wilson's death
   > c. Wilson's idea to reach the summit of Mount Everest

   The article, "Whatever It Takes" begins with _____, goes on to describe _____, and ends with _____.

3. Look for the important ideas and events in paragraphs 9 and 10. Summarize those paragraphs in one or two sentences.

   _____

   _____

   _____

   _____

   _____ Number of correct answers

   Record your personal assessment of your work on the Critical Thinking Chart on page 104.

Critical Thinking

Follow the directions provided for questions 1, 3, and 5. Put an X in the box next to the correct answer for the other questions.

1. For each statement below, write O if it expresses an opinion or write F if it expresses a fact.

   _____ a. Wilson's plan to conquer Mount Everest was ridiculous.

   _____ b. Wilson joined the army on his 18th birthday.

   _____ c. Wilson's trip from England to India in 1933 was more than 5,000 miles long.

2. From the article, you can predict that if Maurice Wilson had been successful, he would have

   ☐ a. joined a monastery.

   ☐ b. attempted to carry out another new and astonishing plan.

   ☐ c. settled into a life of talking about himself.

3. Reread paragraph 6. Then choose from the letters below to correctly complete the following statement. Write the letters on the lines.

According to paragraph 6, _____ happened because _____.

   a. the British government asked airports not to give Wilson any fuel

   b. Wilson was forced to take a longer route

   c. the government of Persia refused to permit use of its airspace

4. From what the article told about one of Wilson's first solo flights, you can conclude that the flight instructor was

   ☐ a. thrilled to have Wilson as a student.

   ☐ b. not a very good teacher.

   ☐ c. amazed that Wilson could complete the difficult flight from England to India.

5. In which paragraph did you find your information or details to answer question 4?

   _____

_____ Number of correct answers

Record your personal assessment of your work on the Critical Thinking Chart on page 104.

Personal Response

This article is different from other articles about climbing Mount Everest I've read because

_____

_____

_____

_____

and Maurice Wilson is unlike other adventurers because

_____

_____

_____

_____

Self-Assessment

While reading this article, I found it easiest to

_____

_____

_____

_____

CRITICAL THINKING

DJ Kool Herc

Hip-Hop Hero

Herc mixed and matched rhythmic beats to create a new musical style.

It's not easy being the new kid in school. It's particularly hard if you're new to the United States, so that everything you say, do, and wear identifies you as an outsider. That was the situation Clive Campbell faced at age 13 when he moved from his native Jamaica to New York City in 1967. From his "roach-killer" boots to the way he pronounced the street names in his new neighborhood, Campbell stood out as different. To fit in, he assimilated the style, customs, and speech patterns of a typical African American teenager from the Bronx. But Campbell didn't forget about the musical traditions and the dance styles of his Jamaican homeland. That turned out to be a very good thing, because Campbell would draw on these heritage styles and blend them with the sounds of the New York music scene. The result turned out to be a breathtaking new style of music now known everywhere in the world as hip-hop.

2   Campbell's music career began in 1973 when his younger sister Cindy organized a back-to-school dance. She asked Campbell to act as the disc jockey, or DJ, for the night, selecting and playing various records throughout the evening. By this time, Campbell had picked up the nickname "Herc" or "Kool Herc"—with "Herc" standing for Hercules because of his big

size and weight-lifting ability. So when Campbell agreed to help his sister out, he used the name "DJ Kool Herc."

3   In preparing for the party, Herc did his homework. He knew the crowd would want to hear lots of funk—the combination of soul, jazz, and rhythm-and-blues that was the most popular sound at the time. He didn't have much money, but he took what he had and bought 20 records, including some that only a few people had heard or were hard to find. He was looking for songs with certain kinds of breaks—short sections where the vocals stop and the instruments take over. Herc wanted breaks with heavy bass and powerful, rhythmic drumming. From his days in Jamaica, he knew that these sections provided the best opportunity for dancing. In Jamaica, reggae records had music and lyrics on one side and instrumental versions on the other. The B-sides were known as "dub" sides or dubplates. As Herc told one reporter, "Every Jamaican record has a dub side to it." He figured that by finding records with energizing "break beats" similar to those on dubplates, he could pump up the crowd. Herc also arranged to use his father's powerful sound system for his sister's party. His father had bought it, but he hadn't known how to hook it up properly. Once Herc got it wired correctly, it produced a sound superior to anything else in the neighborhood.

4   As Herc hoped, everyone at the party loved the funky music and the great sound. They appreciated the fact that his record selection featured break beats that were perfect for dancing. Beyond that, Herc

utilized a technique called "toasting" that he had often witnessed back in Jamaica. DJs were known to call out over the music to various people in the audience. Sometimes DJs threw in a spontaneous poem or a well-known phrase. Herc did the same thing, welcoming friends and acquaintances in local street parlance and adding the occasional rhyme or phrase to the greeting.

As he later put it, "I did a lot of things from Jamaica, and I brought it here and turned it into my own little style." All in all, the night was a huge success, and soon Herc was acting as DJ for parties on a regular basis.

5   Herc's popularity grew in the next few months. A core group of friends showed up at every party, soon becoming known as the "B-boys." It is not clear whether the "B"

A B-boy dances during a three-day international dance battle in Seoul, South Korea.

stood for "beat" or "break" or "B-side," or even "boogie." In any case, Herc could count on the acrobatic footwork of these young men to get the dancing started. "B-boys go down!" he would shout at the start of a break, and they would take over the floor with their increasingly complex set of steps, jumps, and spins. Over time, this form of dancing came to be known as break dancing.

6   Herc was soon hosting all-night dance parties and working in large music clubs. Meanwhile, Herc's calls to the audience were becoming more customized and rhythmic. Often he made up rhymes that contained popular phrases and the slang of the day. Sometimes the rhymes had to do with people he knew in the audience, and people often would shout out their own names in the hope that Herc might mention them. Herc's rhyming dance-party banter was a development that DJs copied and polished to form the rap music of today.

7   While DJ Kool Herc deserves to be remembered for his contributions to rap and break dancing, it is his role as the godfather of hip-hop that classifies him as a true visionary. His inspiration came one

night as he watched people waiting eagerly for one particular break. It occurred to him that he had two or three different records with the same basic beat in the break. How would it be, he wondered, if he strung them together? He decided to give it a whirl, so he told the crowd, "I'm going to try something new tonight. I'm going to call it a merry-go-round." With that said, he proceeded to play the break section of James Brown's "Give It Up Or Turn It Loose" followed by Michael Viner's "Bongo Rock" and then on to Babe Ruth's "The Mexican." The dancers loved it!

8   Even as his reputation grew, Herc kept experimenting. He tried playing a break, then picking the needle up off the record and dropping it back to the beginning of the same break. Herc then found a way to mix the sounds of the two records at the same time by using an audio mixer to jump back and forth between them. In this way, he could play one short break of the song as many times as he wanted. As Herc's fame grew, he decided to focus all of his attention on being a DJ. He got two friends to take over at the microphone while he spun records and mixed the sound. This new

focus made it easy for him to create a new and more complex sound.

9   As other DJs in the Bronx picked up on Herc's innovations, the hip-hop movement grew. Although it didn't get its name for several more years, hip-hop was here to stay. And while many different artists contributed to its growth, it was the "kool" kid from Jamaica who had started it all. ✳

If you have been timed while reading this article, enter your reading time below. Then turn to the Words-per-Minute Table on page 101 and look up your reading speed (words per minute). Enter your reading speed on the graph on page 102.

Reading Time: Lesson 7

_____ : _____

Minutes   Seconds

A Finding the Main Idea

One statement below expresses the main idea of the article. One statement is too general, or too broad. The other statement explains only part of the article; it is too narrow. Label the statements using the following key:

M—Main Idea   **B—Too Broad**   **N—Too Narrow**

_____ 1. The hip-hop movement began in the Bronx.

_____ 2. DJ Kool Herc became famous for his contributions to rap, break dancing, and hip-hop music.

_____ 3. Clive Campbell, known as DJ Kool Herc, began his musical career at a dance in 1973.

_____ Score 15 points for a correct M answer.

_____ Score 5 points for each correct B or N answer.

_____ **Total Score**: Finding the Main Idea

B Recalling Facts

How well do you remember the facts in the article? Put an X in the box next to the answer that correctly completes each statement about the article.

1. Clive Campbell moved to New York from
    □ a. the Dominican Republic.
    □ b. Haiti.
    □ c. Jamaica.

2. Campbell came to the United States when he was
    □ a. 5 years old.
    □ b. 13 years old.
    □ c. 17 years old.

3. Breaks in songs were good for
    □ a. dancing.
    □ b. taking a break and resting.
    □ c. calling out to the audience.

4. The dub sides of records were sides with
    □ a. sound effects added.
    □ b. mistakes on them.
    □ c. instrumental versions of songs.

5. When a DJ calls out to the crowd, the DJ is
    □ a. rapping.
    □ b. toasting.
    □ c. breaking.

Score 5 points for each correct answer.

_____ **Total Score**: Recalling Facts

C Making Inferences

When you combine your own experiences and information from a text to draw a conclusion that is not directly stated in that text, you are making an inference. Below are five statements that may or may not be inferences based on information in the article. Label the statements using the following key:

C—Correct Inference   **F—Faulty Inference**

_____ 1. Herc did not have any original ideas; he just copied the customs of his native country.

_____ 2. Herc was an outgoing man who enjoyed being with and talking to people.

_____ 3. What happened in the New York music scene had a great influence on music in the rest of the country.

_____ 4. Herc was the only DJ in New York City when he started.

_____ 5. Herc liked a variety of music styles.

> Score 5 points for each correct answer.
>
> _____ **Total Score**: Making Inferences

D Using Words Precisely

Each numbered sentence below contains an underlined word or phrase from the article. Following the sentence are three definitions. One definition is closest to the meaning of the underlined word. One definition is opposite or nearly opposite. Label those two definitions using the following key. Do not label the remaining definition.

C—Closest   **O—Opposite or Nearly Opposite**

1. To fit in, Campbell <u>assimilated</u> the style, customs, and speech patterns of a typical teenager from the Bronx.

_____ a. rejected, did not accept

_____ b. made fun of, mocked

_____ c. took on as one's own, absorbed

2. Herc <u>utilized</u> a technique called "toasting" that he had seen back in his native land.

_____ a. remembered

_____ b. made use of

_____ c. left alone, ignored

3. Herc called out to people in the audience and sometimes threw in <u>spontaneous</u> poems or sayings.

_____ a. unprepared, made up at the moment

_____ b. planned, rehearsed

_____ c. humorous, comical

4. Herc welcomed friends and acquaintances in local street <u>parlance</u> and added an occasional rhyme or phrase to the greeting.

_____ a. loud volume

_____ b. style or manner of speaking

_____ c. signals or silent motions

5. Meanwhile, Herc's calls to the audience were becoming more <u>customized</u> and rhythmic.

_____ a. previously used

_____ b. very unusual

_____ c. original; made to order

_____ Score 3 points for each correct C answer.

_____ Score 2 points for each correct O answer.

_____ **Total Score**: Using Words Precisely

Enter the four total scores in the spaces below, and add them together to find your Reading Comprehension Score. Then record your score on the graph on page 103.

Score	Question Type	Lesson 7
_____	Finding the Main Idea	
_____	Recalling Facts	
_____	Making Inferences	
_____	Using Words Precisely	
_____	**Reading Comprehension Score**	

Author's Approach

Put an X in the box next to the correct answer.

1. The main purpose of the first paragraph is to

☐ a. make DJ Kool Herc's background clear to the reader.

☐ b. describe the problems Herc had when he came to the United States.

☐ c. inform the reader about different musical traditions.

2. From the statements below, choose two that you believe the author would agree with.

☐ a. DJ Kool Herc was a creative man.

☐ b. DJ Kool Herc created a popular new style of dance music.

☐ c. DJ Kool Herc did not know anything about music, but he knew what people liked.

3. The author tells this story mainly by

☐ a. describing the dance music scene in New York in the 1970s.

☐ b. explaining the changes Herc introduced to the New York dance music scene.

☐ c. showing how rap music was started.

4. In this article, "In preparing for the party, Herc did his homework" means

☐ a. Herc took his job at the party seriously and worked hard to get ready.

☐ b. Herc used part of his homework in his preparation for the party.

☐ c. Herc did his homework while listening to the records he would bring to the party.

_____ Number of correct answers

Record your personal assessment of your work on the Critical Thinking Chart on page 104.

Summarizing and Paraphrasing

Put an X next to the correct answer for questions 1 and 2. Follow the directions provided for question 3.

1. Read the statement from the article below. Then read the paraphrase of that statement. Choose the reason that best tells why the paraphrase does not say the same thing as the statement.

   Statement: Herc's inspiration came one night as he watched people waiting eagerly for one particular break.

   Paraphrase: One night, Herc came up with a great idea.

   ☐ a.   Paraphrase says too much.

   ☐ b.   Paraphrase doesn't say enough.

   ☐ c.   Paraphrase doesn't agree with the statement.

2. Choose the sentence that correctly restates the following sentence from the article: "Even as his reputation grew, Herc kept experimenting."

   ☐ a.   Because Herc was famous, he started to experiment.

   ☐ b.   Though he was well-known, Herc never stopped doing his best.

   ☐ c.   As Herc became more popular, he kept trying new things.

3. Look for the important ideas and events in paragraphs 5 and 6. Summarize those paragraphs in one or two sentences.

   _____

   _____

   _____

   _____

_____   Number of correct answers

Record your personal assessment of your work on the Critical Thinking Chart on page 104.

Critical Thinking

Put an X next to the correct answer for questions 1, 3, 4, and 5. Follow the directions provided for question 2.

1. From what the article told about music, you can predict that

   ☐ a.   no other style of music will ever be more popular than hip-hop.

   ☐ b.   hip-hop was the first kind of dance music.

   ☐ c.   new styles of music will be created that will feature some form of hip-hop.

2. Reread paragraph 2. Then choose from the letters below to correctly complete the following statement. Write the letters on the lines.

   According to paragraph 2, _____ because _____.

   a.   Campbell was a big, strong guy

   b.   he took the name "DJ Kool Herc"

   c.   friends started calling Campbell "Herc," short for "Hercules"

3. How is "DJ Kool Herc" an example of the theme of *Visionaries*?

   ☐ a.   Herc could imagine approaches to music that had never been tried before.

   ☐ b.   Herc chose music that pleased a lot of people.

   ☐ c.   Herc was very knowledgeable about music.

4. If you were a DJ, how could you use the information in the article to gain a wider reputation in the music scene?

   ☐ a.   Give the people what they are used to hearing and what they already like.

   ☐ b.   Come up with new ideas and experiment with new sounds.

   ☐ c.   Get a "kool" nickname.

5. What did you have to do to answer question 4?

☐ a. find a comparison (how things are the same)

☐ b. find a fact (something that you can prove is true)

☐ c. draw a conclusion (a sensible statement based on the text and your experience)

_____ Number of correct answers

Record your personal assessment of your work on the Critical Thinking Chart on page 104.

Personal Response

One good question about this article that was not asked would be

_____

_____

_____

_____

_____

_____

Self-Assessment

Before reading the article, I already knew

_____

_____

_____

_____

_____

_____

_____

_____

_____

_____

_____

_____

Lucy

An Experiment

Dr. Roger Fouts teaches Lucy American Sign Language.

Lucy was just two days old when she was taken from her birth mother, wrapped in a baby blanket and placed in a bassinet. She was carried onto a plane and flown from Tarpon Springs, Florida, to Norman, Oklahoma. There she joined the family of Jane and Maurice K. Temerlin and their 11-year-old son, Steve. Adoptions were not uncommon in 1964, but this one was different. That's because little Lucy Temerlin was an ape.

2   In scientific evolutionary terms, apes are considered the closest species to humans. Scientific studies have shown that apes and humans share at least 96 percent of the same DNA. Maurice Temerlin was a behavioral scientist who wanted to test the theory that nature is stronger than nurture. In other words, he wanted to know if our behavior is controlled by what we are—our species—or by how we live and our surroundings. Temerlin believed the only way to find out was to raise Lucy not as a pet, but as a *human* member of their family. The results would benefit the research at the University of Oklahoma's Institute for Primate Studies, where Temerlin was associated. In his excitement to conduct this experiment, Temerlin was focused on how much science would gain. Probably no one thought to ask how much Lucy had to lose.

3   Lucy was born into a colony of carnival chimpanzees and spent her first two days of life surrounded by other chimps. But from the moment her owner sold her to the Institute for Primate Studies, she lived exclusively in the company of humans. Jane and Maurice Temerlin fed Lucy with a baby bottle, dressed her in diapers and baby clothes, and laid her down each night in a crib in their bedroom. As Lucy grew, they fed her in a high chair and then taught her to eat at the table using a fork, knife, and spoon. When she got too big for her crib, they let her sleep in their bed with them. Lucy was taught to communicate in American Sign Language, in which she learned 140 signs. When the Temerlins took her to the doctor for check-ups, they went to a pediatrician rather than a veterinarian, and they also made sure Lucy received vaccinations for childhood diseases just as human children would. In short, the couple did all that they could to filter the animal out of the ape.

4   From the Temerlins' point of view, the experiment proceeded beautifully for several years. Lucy played with human toys, ate three scheduled meals a day, and learned to use a variety of tools, such as a screwdriver, a vacuum cleaner, and locks. She spent half the day studying sign language. The rest of the day was spent doing as she pleased—flipping through magazines, watching television, playing with her pet kitten, or going fishing with Maurice Temerlin. Reporters who visited the home were often greeted at the door by Lucy, who then would hurry into the kitchen and make tea for the guests.

5   By the time Lucy was 10, the situation had begun to change. Lucy became harder to manage. Full-grown chimps are not bigger than humans, but they are about five times as strong. When Lucy became angry, she did more than throw a tantrum—she turned into a destroying menace. In addition, Lucy was increasingly interested in finding a mate. Since her only contact was with humans, she started to show physical attraction toward human males, particularly toward Maurice Temerlin. For the next couple of years, Lucy became harder and harder to control, careening around the house, breaking things, and occasionally even biting people. In the words of one reporter, she was "tearing the house to shreds." The Temerlins blocked off part of their living quarters and put Lucy in a padded room with bars so she couldn't

In this family photo, Jane Temerlin and her "child" spend some quality time.

get out. But by 1977, when Lucy was 12, the Temerlins decided they had had enough. As Maurice Temerlin explained it, he and his wife wanted to "live normal lives now."

6   Getting Lucy out of their lives may have been a good thing for Jane and Maurice Temerlin, but it was the worst thing that could happen for Lucy. She knew no life other than the one she had with them. The Temerlins decided not to put her in a private colony like the one she had been born into because they thought it would be too limiting for her. They also rejected research labs and zoos as being too sterile and boring. Instead, they decided to turn her loose in the wild. They chose a chimpanzee sanctuary in Gambia, Africa, where chimps that had been kept in zoos, circuses, or private homes could be set free. Before the Temerlins flew Lucy to Gambia to release her, they hired a graduate student in psychology named Janis Carter to come with them. The Temerlins stayed in Gambia only a short time, and then they left Carter there to help Lucy get used to living free in the wild.

7   For the first time ever in her life, Lucy had to look out for herself. Instead of having her own room and a closet full of clothes, Lucy was surrounded by trees. Instead of eating casseroles and sipping lemonade, she was expected to forage for

leaves and drink from a stream. It was too much for her all at once, and she refused. She would not climb trees, build a nest, or interact with the other chimps. She often sat dejectedly, pulling out her hair, and signing to Carter the same message: "Lucy's hurt."

8   Carter had intended to stay only two weeks after the Temerlins left, but Lucy was obviously so confused that Carter couldn't bear to leave. She actually stayed with Lucy for several years, working to get her to become less human and more like an ape. Carter demonstrated to Lucy which foods she should eat and how to find them. She communicated with Lucy only through ape-like vocal sounds, not through sign language. Finally, Carter's work began to pay off. Lucy showed signs of adapting to her natural habitat, and Carter believed Lucy could learn to live by herself.

9   After nearly eight years, Carter left the chimpanzee sanctuary, staying away a full six months before checking on Lucy again. When Carter did return, she brought Lucy's mirror and several other things that had been part of Lucy's life with the Temerlins. Lucy welcomed Carter and played briefly with the items, then turned and rejoined the other chimps. Carter rejoiced in this hopeful sign that Lucy had successfully integrated into ape society.

10   Unfortunately, this triumph was short lived. Less than a year later, Lucy's lifeless body was found in the open with her hands and feet missing. Although no one is certain what happened, Carter thinks that poachers had entered the sanctuary and Lucy, who had long ago learned to trust humans, had walked up to greet them. Carter guessed that they had taken Lucy's hands and feet as trophies from their hunt. It was a tragic end for a creature whose life was sacrificed to the vision of well-meaning but single-minded researchers who only wanted to learn why we humans behave as we do. ✳

If you have been timed while reading this article, enter your reading time below. Then turn to the Words-per-Minute Table on page 101 and look up your reading speed (words per minute). Enter your reading speed on the graph on page 102.

Reading Time: Lesson 8

_____ : _____
Minutes   *Seconds*

A | Finding the Main Idea

One statement below expresses the main idea of the article. One statement is too general, or too broad. The other statement explains only part of the article; it is too narrow. Label the statements using the following key:

M—Main Idea   **B—Too Broad**   **N—Too Narrow**

_____ 1. Chimps and humans are actually quite similar in many ways.

_____ 2. Jane and Maurice Temerlin put their chimp Lucy in a chimpanzee sanctuary in Gambia, where they hoped she would adapt to living in the wild.

_____ 3. Jane and Maurice Temerlin raised a chimp they called Lucy as a human for 12 years to see whether nature or nurture controls behavior.

_____ Score 15 points for a correct M answer.

_____ Score 5 points for each correct B or N answer.

_____ **Total Score**: Finding the Main Idea

B | Recalling Facts

How well do you remember the facts in the article? Put an X in the box next to the answer that correctly completes each statement about the article.

1. Maurice Temerlin was a
   ☐ a. behavioral scientist.
   ☐ b. zoo keeper.
   ☐ c. high school teacher.

2. The Temerlins taught Lucy to communicate in
   ☐ a. ape grunts.
   ☐ b. very simple English.
   ☐ c. American Sign Language.

3. The Temerlins eventually had to put Lucy in a
   ☐ a. padded room with bars.
   ☐ b. cage in the basement.
   ☐ c. backyard house.

4. Janis Carter stayed on to help Lucy for
   ☐ a. about six months.
   ☐ b. exactly one year.
   ☐ c. almost eight years.

5. Carter believes that Lucy was killed by
   ☐ a. other apes who were jealous of her.
   ☐ b. poachers hunting on the chimpanzee sanctuary.
   ☐ c. the owners of the chimpanzee sanctuary.

Score 5 points for each correct answer.

_____ **Total Score**: Recalling Facts

C Making Inferences

When you combine your own experiences and information from a text to draw a conclusion that is not directly stated in that text, you are making an inference. Below are five statements that may or may not be inferences based on information in the article. Label the statements using the following key:

C—Correct Inference   **F—Faulty Inference**

_____ 1. The Temerlins likely were strong supporters of animal rights.

_____ 2. Janis Carter did not realize at first how involved she would become with Lucy.

_____ 3. Lucy probably would have been happier if she had been raised with other chimps.

_____ 4. The Temerlins treated Lucy well while she was living in their home.

_____ 5. Lucy was more intelligent than most chimps.

Score 5 points for each correct answer.

_____ **Total Score**: Making Inferences

D Using Words Precisely

Each numbered sentence below contains an underlined word or phrase from the article. Following the sentence are three definitions. One definition is closest to the meaning of the underlined word. One definition is opposite or nearly opposite. Label those two definitions using the following key. Do not label the remaining definition.

C—Closest   **O—Opposite or Nearly Opposite**

1. But from the moment her owner sold her to the Institute for Primate Studies, she lived <u>exclusively</u> in the company of humans.

    _____ a. privately

    _____ b. entirely

    _____ c. partially

2. For the next couple of years, Lucy became harder and harder to control, <u>careening</u> around the house, breaking things, occasionally even biting people.

    _____ a. rushing carelessly

    _____ b. living alone

    _____ c. moving slowly and carefully

3. They also rejected research labs and zoos as being too <u>sterile</u> and boring.

    _____ a. exciting and lively

    _____ b. lacking variety or creativity

    _____ c. unfamiliar

4. She refused to eat, climb trees, build a nest, or <u>interact</u> with the other chimps.

    _____ a. join with socially

    _____ b. recognize

    _____ c. keep away from

5. Carter rejoiced in this hopeful sign that Lucy had successfully <u>integrated into</u> ape society.

_____ a. learned about

_____ b. separated from

_____ c. become a part of

_____ Score 3 points for each correct C answer.

_____ Score 2 points for each correct O answer.

_____ **Total Score**: Using Words Precisely

Enter the four total scores in the spaces below, and add them together to find your Reading Comprehension Score. Then record your score on the graph on page 103.

Score	Question Type	Lesson 8
_____	Finding the Main Idea	
_____	Recalling Facts	
_____	Making Inferences	
_____	Using Words Precisely	
_____	**Reading Comprehension Score**	

Author's Approach

Put an X in the box next to the correct answer.

1. How is the author's purpose for writing the article expressed in paragraph 2?

☐ a. This paragraph states that humans and chimps share at least 96 percent of the same DNA.

☐ b. This paragraph states that Maurice Temerlin wanted to conduct a long-term experiment.

☐ c. This paragraph points out that the Temerlins did not think about what would be best for Lucy.

2. The author tells this story mainly by

☐ a. comparing different topics.

☐ b. using their imagination or creativity.

☐ c. describing events in the order they happened.

3. Which of the following statements from the article best describes why the Temerlins decided to release Lucy to a chimpanzee sanctuary?

☐ a. "For the next couple of years, Lucy became harder and harder to control, careening around the house, breaking things, occasionally even biting people."

☐ b. "Getting Lucy out of their lives may have been a good thing for Jane and Maurice Temerlin, but it was the worst thing that could happen for Lucy."

☐ c. "Jane and Maurice Temerlin fed Lucy with a baby bottle, dressed her in diapers and baby clothes, and laid her down each night in a crib in their bedroom."

_____ Number of correct answers

Record your personal assessment of your work on the Critical Thinking Chart on page 104.

CRITICAL THINKING

Summarizing and Paraphrasing

Put an X in the box next to the correct answer.

1. Choose the best one-sentence paraphrase for the following sentence from the article: "Carter had intended to stay only two weeks after the Temerlins left, but Lucy was obviously so confused that Carter couldn't bear to leave."

   ☐ a. The Temerlins left after only two weeks, but Carter stayed on because she saw that Lucy was confused.

   ☐ b. Although she had planned on leaving only two weeks after the Temerlins, Carter decided to stay after seeing how confused Lucy was.

   ☐ c. Carter stayed with Lucy for two weeks after the Temerlins left because she saw that the chimp was unbearably confused.

2. Below are summaries of the article. Choose the summary that says all the most important things about the article but in the fewest words.

   ☐ a. The Temerlin family raised a chimp as a human to see what makes us who we are—our species or how we are treated. Years later, when the chimp became hard to manage, they released her in Africa. She was killed, probably by poachers she had trusted.

   ☐ b. Maurice Temerlin wondered whether it is our species or how we are treated that makes us who we are. His family took in a baby chimp and raised it as a human for 12 years. Then they released her, and she was killed.

   ☐ c. Maurice and Jane Temerlin raised a chimp as a human. By the time she was 12 years old, she became hard to handle, so they released her into the wild.

   ___ Number of correct answers

   Record your personal assessment of your work on the Critical Thinking Chart on page 104.

Critical Thinking

Put an X in the box next to the correct answer for questions 1, 3, and 4. Follow the directions provided for question 2.

1. Which of the following statements from the article is an opinion rather than a fact?

   ☐ a. "Full-grown chimps are not bigger than humans, but they are about five times as strong."

   ☐ b. "In short, the Temerlins did all that they could to filter the animal out of the ape."

   ☐ c. "For the first time ever in her life, Lucy had to look out for herself."

2. Choose from the letters below to correctly complete the following statement. Write the letter on the lines.

   On the positive side, _____, but on the negative side _____.

   a. Lucy had a very difficult time fitting in with other apes in the wild because of the experiment

   b. the experiment successfully proved that a chimp could learn many of the skills that a human child learns

   c. as part of the experiment, Lucy was cared for by a pediatrician, not a veterinarian

3. What was the effect of Lucy's release into the wild?

   ☐ a. She became sad and refused to care for herself or socialize.

   ☐ b. She became angry and lashed out at Carter.

   ☐ c. She was relieved at being given her freedom.

4. What did you have to do to answer question 2?

☐ a. find a cause (why something happened)

☐ b. find a contrast (how things are different)

☐ c. find an opinion (what someone thinks about something)

_____ Number of correct answers

Record your personal assessment of your work on the Critical Thinking Chart on page 104.

Personal Response

A question I would like answered by Janis Carter is

_____

_____

_____

_____

_____

_____

Self-Assessment

Which concepts or ideas from the article were difficult to understand?

_____

_____

_____

_____

_____

_____

Which were easy?

_____

_____

_____

_____

_____

_____

_____

Wrapped Up in Their Art

The Gates *is the largest public arts project in the history of New York.*

"I can't promise, particularly since this is New York, that everyone will love *The Gates*, but I guarantee that they will all talk about it," proclaimed New York City Mayor Michael Bloomberg in 2005. "And that's really what innovative, provocative art is supposed to do."

2   The mayor was right on both counts. *The Gates* was not universally loved. Some people called it a "work of art," "poetry in motion," and "a holy place to walk." Others condemned it as "ugly," "insane," and "a waste of money." Still, people who visited *The Gates* in Central Park couldn't seem to stop talking about this unique creation by visionary artists Christo and Jeanne-Claude. Creating art that both shocked and amazed is what the couple had done for decades. Their creations had always been for the sake of art and nothing else. As Jeanne-Claude explained, "Our art has absolutely no purpose, except to be a work of art. We do not give messages."

3   Unlike other visual artists who paint, carve, or sculpt, Christo and Jeanne-Claude specialized in creating works of art on a vast scale. They became famous by wrapping buildings, monuments, bridges, and geographical landmarks with plastic and fabric. Since their projects were usually massive and were created in public places, it often took them several years from conceiving an idea until they received the necessary permission and were able to complete a work. For example, they first envisioned *The Gates* in 1979, but the New York City Parks Department rejected it in 1981. It wasn't until 2003 that Mayor Bloomberg's administration approved the project. The work was displayed in 2005, and the title was "The Gates, Central Park, New York, 1979–2005."

4   *The Gates* consisted of 7,503 vinyl gates, each one 16 feet high and each with pleated, orange-colored nylon drapes blowing in the breeze. The flowing gates stretched for 23 miles along Central Park's winding walkways. Michael Kimmelman, writing in the *New York Times*, described *The Gates* as "a long, billowy saffron ribbon meandering through Central Park." Viewed from nearby buildings, it looked like a shimmering orange river. From ground level in Central Park it was like walking under a flowing golden ceiling.

5   For the critics who found *The Gates* unattractive or offensive, there was not much to say in its defense. Everyone is entitled to an opinion, especially when it comes to something as subjective as modern art. But to those who said it was a "waste of money," the point could be made that at least it was Christo and Jeanne-Claude's own money. The pair put up the entire $20 million it took to buy the materials and pay the thousands of workers who labored on the project. Christo and Jeanne-Claude made most of that money by selling to art collectors the original rough drawings, scale models, and other works of preparation from their various projects.

6   *The Gates* attracted more than 5 million people. This stunning display, which took so much time and money to construct, lasted just 16 days. After that, the work was taken apart and all the building materials recycled. Christo and Jeanne-Claude intended their art to be temporary; they wanted it to make its mark on the public mind and then disappear.

7   Like some other famous artists, Christo and Jeanne-Claude were known just by their first names. By coincidence, they were both born in the same hour on the exact same day—June 13, 1935. Christo was born

Christo and Jeanne-Claude talk about one of their projects.

in Bulgaria and Jeanne-Claude was born in Morocco, and they met and fell in love in Paris in 1958. Soon after that, they began sharing their artistic vision of wrapping very large things. They were married in 1962, and two years after that, the couple settled in New York. They traveled all over the world to construct their works of art. They first gained worldwide fame in 1972 when they suspended a 400-yard curtain across a valley in Colorado. Then, in 1976, they presented *Running Fence* in California, a series of fabric panels that ran 24 miles. The "fence" appeared to flow across the countryside until it disappeared into the ocean.

8   "Every project is a slice of our lives, a particular moment in our lives, and we'll never do it again," Christo said later about the project. "This is an absolutely unique image, meaning there will be no other *Running Fence*, no other *Gates*, no other *Valley Curtain*, no other *Surrounded Islands*." Christo and Jeanne-Claude never accepted money for their works or their ideas, nor did they charge admission to experience them. The reason they were so adamant about not taking donations and payments was because they wanted to keep their art free from outside influence. They felt that if they allowed someone to help pay for materials and labor, they would also be required to listen and accept his or her ideas for the art.

9   Not everyone understood or appreciated what Christo and Jeanne-Claude were trying to do. For example, it took them nine years to persuade the mayor of Paris to let them drape fabric over Pont Neuf, the city's oldest bridge. Finally, in 1985, they wrapped the bridge with more than 450,000 square feet of fabric that was held together by nearly 43,000 feet of rope. In 1995 they wrapped the Reichstag, a famous government building in Berlin, Germany. The artists worked with 90 professional climbers and 120 installation workers for three months wrapping the landmark. All in all, it took about a million square feet of fireproof polypropylene fabric, 51,000 feet of blue rope, and 200 metric tons of steel. Before any of the work was done, the artists had to present their ideas to the members of the German parliament and also make several telephone calls. Even after that, the officials still argued for 70-minutes before a vote was called and the parliament approved the two-week display.

10   Perhaps their most ambitious and expensive work of art was the 1991 *Umbrella* project. Christo and Jeanne-Claude, along with 1,880 workers, installed 1,340 blue umbrellas in an inland river valley in Japan. They also put up 1,760 yellow umbrellas in an inland dry valley in California. The blue represented the abundance of water at the Japanese location and the yellow stood for the heat of the California valley. Each umbrella was 19 feet 8 inches high and 28 feet 6 inches in diameter. On October 9, workers on both sides of the Pacific Ocean opened all the umbrellas at the same time. The public viewed the presentation for 18 days before it was taken down and recycled.

11   Although these works of art were temporary, the impression they made on the minds of many viewers lasted a long time. Before Jeanne-Claude's death in 2009, she and Christo liked to say that they intervened in the lives of the local people only to create "gentle disturbances." He will continue their goal of giving people a brand new way to look at familiar surroundings. Christo always liked the expression "Once upon a time." He told a reporter that he likes to imagine someone is walking through Central Park at this very moment and thinking, "Once upon a time, *The Gates* were here." ✳

If you have been timed while reading this article, enter your reading time below. Then turn to the Words-per-Minute Table on page 101 and look up your reading speed (words per minute). Enter your reading speed on the graph on page 102.

Reading Time: Lesson 9

_____ : _____
Minutes   *Seconds*

A Finding the Main Idea

One statement below expresses the main idea of the article. One statement is too general, or too broad. The other statement explains only part of the article; it is too narrow. Label the statements using the following key:

M—Main Idea   **B—Too Broad**   **N—Too Narrow**

_____ 1. Christo and Jeanne-Claude created massive works of art all around the world and then took them apart after only a few weeks.

_____ 2. Christo and Jeanne-Claude created *The Gates*, a huge work of art in New York's Central Park.

_____ 3. Christo and Jeanne-Claude were different from most other visual artists.

_____ Score 15 points for a correct M answer.

_____ Score 5 points for each correct B or N answer.

_____ **Total Score**: Finding the Main Idea

B Recalling Facts

How well do you remember the facts in the article? Put an X in the box next to the answer that correctly completes each statement about the article.

1. *The Gates* was displayed in New York's Central Park in
   - ☐ a. 1979.
   - ☐ b. 2003.
   - ☐ c. 2005.

2. Christo and Jeanne-Claude first gained worldwide fame for suspending a 400-yard curtain across a valley in
   - ☐ a. Bulgaria.
   - ☐ b. Colorado.
   - ☐ c. California.

3. In 1985 the artists wrapped in fabric the oldest bridge in
   - ☐ a. Berlin, Germany.
   - ☐ b. Tangier, Morocco.
   - ☐ c. Paris, France.

4. The *Umbrella* project lasted
   - ☐ a. 16 days.
   - ☐ b. 18 days.
   - ☐ c. 2 weeks.

5. The umbrellas in the *Umbrella* project were
   - ☐ a. blue and yellow.
   - ☐ b. blue and orange.
   - ☐ c. yellow and green.

Score 5 points for each correct answer.

_____ **Total Score**: Recalling Facts

C Making Inferences

When you combine your own experiences and information from a text to draw a conclusion that is not directly stated in that text, you are making an inference. Below are five statements that may or may not be inferences based on information in the article. Label the statements using the following key:

C—Correct Inference   **F—Faulty Inference**

_____ 1. Some people wish Christo and Jeanne-Claude's art works were not temporary.

_____ 2. For the *Umbrella* project, workers in Japan and California opened the umbrellas at the same time only once during the entire display period.

_____ 3. The majority of art critics do not admire the works of Christo and Jeanne-Claude.

_____ 4. Christo and Jeanne-Claude were difficult to work with.

_____ 5. Authorities hesitate to give permission for Christo and Jeanne-Claude's art projects because they are concerned the art works might cause damage.

Score 5 points for each correct answer.

_____ **Total Score**: Making Inferences

D Using Words Precisely

Each numbered sentence below contains an underlined word or phrase from the article. Following the sentence are three definitions. One definition is closest to the meaning of the underlined word. One definition is opposite or nearly opposite. Label those two definitions using the following key. Do not label the remaining definition.

C—Closest   **O—Opposite or Nearly Opposite**

1. People talked about *The Gates* because it was underlined provocative art.

   _____ a. made from heavy materials

   _____ b. stimulating, exciting

   _____ c. ordinary

2. Michael Kimmelman, writing in the *New York Times*, described *The Gates* as "a long, billowy saffron ribbon."

   _____ a. firm and straight

   _____ b. foolish, ridiculous

   _____ c. wavy, rising and falling

3. Everyone is entitled to an opinion when it comes to something as subjective as modern art.

   _____ a. based on feelings rather than fact

   _____ b. objective, neutral

   _____ c. new, up-to-date

4. Christo and Jeanne-Claude were adamant about not taking outside donations and payments.

   _____ a. criticized, blamed

   _____ b. flexible, willing to change

   _____ c. firmly decided, determined

5. Christo and Jeanne-Claude <u>intervened in</u> the lives of local people only to create "gentle disturbances."

_____ a. became involved with

_____ b. got excited by

_____ c. sent away from

_____ Score 3 points for each correct C answer.

_____ Score 2 points for each correct O answer.

_____ **Total Score**: Using Words Precisely

Enter the four total scores in the spaces below, and add them together to find your Reading Comprehension Score. Then record your score on the graph on page 103.

Score	Question Type	Lesson 9
_____	Finding the Main Idea	
_____	Recalling Facts	
_____	Making Inferences	
_____	Using Words Precisely	
_____	**Reading Comprehension Score**	

Author's Approach

Put an X in the box next to the correct answer.

1. The author probably wrote this article to
   ☐ a. express an opinion about Christo and Jeanne-Claude.
   ☐ b. introduce the reader to the original art works of Christo and Jeanne-Claude.
   ☐ c. describe one popular form of modern art.

2. The author tells this story mainly by
   ☐ a. describing some of the artists' major works of art.
   ☐ b. listing events of the artists' lives in chronological order.
   ☐ c. discussing the obstacles Christo and Jeanne-Claude faced in bringing their artistic visions to life.

3. What does the author imply by saying "Viewed from nearby buildings, The Gates looked like a shimmering orange river"?
   ☐ a. The Gates was strange and looked out-of-place in a park.
   ☐ b. The Gates were orange and followed a winding path through the park.
   ☐ c. Viewers of The Gates were confused by what the artists meant.

4. Judging by statements from the article "Wrapped Up in Their Art," you can conclude that the author wants the reader to think that
   ☐ a. Christo and Jeanne-Claude were builders, not real artists.
   ☐ b. the artists did their best with the money they could raise.
   ☐ c. Christo and Jeanne-Claude were fully dedicated to their art.

_____ Number of correct answers

Record your personal assessment of your work on the Critical Thinking Chart on page 104.

CRITICAL THINKING

Summarizing and Paraphrasing

Put an X in the box next to the correct answer for questions 1 and 2. Follow the directions provided for question 3.

1. Read the statement from the article below. Then read the paraphrase of that statement. Choose the reason that best tells why the paraphrase does not say the same thing as the statement.

   Statement: Like some other famous artists, Christo and Jeanne-Claude were known by their first names only.

   Paraphrase: Everyone called Christo and Jeanne-Claude by their first names because they were famous artists.

   ☐ a.   Paraphrase says too much.

   ☐ b.   Paraphrase doesn't say enough.

   ☐ c.   Paraphrase doesn't agree with the statement.

2. Choose the sentence that correctly restates the following sentence from the article: "Christo and Jeanne-Claude intended their art to be temporary; they wanted it to make its mark on the public mind and then disappear."

   ☐ a.   Christo and Jeanne-Claude wanted their work of art to last a short time.

   ☐ b.   Christo and Jeanne-Claude wanted their work of art to make an impression on the public for the short time that it was displayed.

   ☐ c.   Christo and Jeanne-Claude wanted their work of art to last a short time until they disappeared.

3. Reread paragraph 10 in the article. Below, write a summary of the paragraph in no more than 15 words.

   _____

   _____

   _____

   _____

   Reread your summary and decide whether it covers the important ideas in the paragraph. Next, decide how to shorten the summary to 15 words or less without leaving out any essential information. Write this summary below.

   _____

   _____

   _____

   _____

   _____ Number of correct answers

   Record your personal assessment of your work on the Critical Thinking Chart on page 104.

Critical Thinking

Follow the directions provided for questions 1 and 3. Put an X next to the correct answer for the other questions.

1. For each statement below, write O if it expresses an opinion or write F if it expresses a fact.

   _____ a.   *The Gates* was a waste of money.

   _____ b.   *The Gates* was not universally loved.

   _____ c.   *The Gates* was poetry in motion.

2. From the article, you can predict that if Christo continues to plan and raise money for massive art works,

☐ a. he will have to persuade more authorities to give permission for the projects.

☐ b. he will make the works of art permanent.

☐ c. everyone will love and appreciate his creations.

3. Reread paragraph 3. Then choose from the letters below to correctly complete the following statement. Write the letters on the lines.

According to paragraph 3, _____ because _____.

a. New York authorities would not give permission to construct it

b. it took 26 years to complete *The Gates*

c. the artists were famous for wrapping landmarks

4. Of the following theme categories, which would this story fit into?

☐ a. Art of the 21st Century

☐ b. The World's Landmarks

☐ c. Modern Artists

5. From what the article told about Christo and Jeanne-Claude, you can conclude that they

☐ a. did not have many ideas for works of art.

☐ b. probably enjoyed surprising and amazing people.

☐ c. were not respected in the art world.

_____ Number of correct answers

Record your personal assessment of your work on the Critical Thinking Chart on page 104.

Personal Response

What would you say if Christo wanted to make your yard or your home a temporary work of art?

_____

_____

_____

_____

Self-Assessment

One of the things I did best when reading this article was

_____

_____

_____

_____

I believe I did this well because

_____

_____

_____

_____

CRITICAL THINKING

Mark Zuckerberg

Making Friends

Mark Zuckerberg, left, and Chris Hughes were students at Harvard University when they created Facebook.

In 2003 a lot of people were angry at 19-year-old Harvard University student Mark Zuckerberg. His computer prank nearly got him expelled from school. Today, however, when people think of Mark Zuckerberg, it's because of the social networking Web site he created—Facebook—and the major impact the site has had on the lives of people all over the world.

2   Zuckerberg began writing computer programs when he was in the sixth grade. Most of his knowledge came from sharing ideas with friends who were also interested in computers. His local high school didn't offer enough high-level math or computer classes, so he transferred to Phillips Exeter Academy, one of the top private schools in the country. As a senior, he and classmate Adam D'Angelo developed an imaginative computer program called Synapse as part of a project requirement for graduation. Basically, they built a plug-in device for an MP3 player that would gather a person's preferences in music and then create a playlist to meet that taste. They posted it as a free download on the Internet, and soon major computer companies were calling them with offers of jobs and money for the rights to sell it. "Some companies offered us right off the bat up to $1 million," said Zuckerberg. However, the boys turned down all of it. They had their eyes firmly on the future, and that meant going to college.

3   It was during his sophomore year at Harvard that Zuckerberg's life got really interesting. At the time, the university did not have a computerized student directory with photos and basic background information as other colleges did. Such a directory was commonly called a "face book," and it enabled classmates to learn about each other quickly and easily online. Zuckerberg wanted to compile something similar for undergraduates at Harvard, but the school administrators were slow to get the idea organized. "They kept on saying that there were all these reasons why they couldn't aggregate this information," he said.

4   Zuckerberg wanted to prove that the information could be gathered. He hacked into Harvard's protected student records and copied all of the students' ID photos. However, instead of setting up a student directory, Zuckerberg created a Web site he called "Facemash," on which he randomly paired photos of undergraduates. Then he invited fellow students to visit the site and vote on which student was "hotter" by clicking the mouse. In just four hours, the site went viral, with 450 visitors and 22,000 photo views. When school officials found out about Facemash, they shut down Zuckerberg's Internet connection. Many students were mad about Facemash too. A lot of them complained about having their images displayed without their knowledge or consent. They felt humiliated being compared to others—and they *really* didn't like having their "hotness" judged on the basis of a college ID photo. Even so, many students couldn't seem to look away. Rebecca Davis O'Brien, who was a student at Harvard at the time, wrote in 2010 that clicking through Facemash filled her with a kind of "Internet ickiness." She said it combined the excitement of an anonymous chat room with the meanness of a slam book. "It was callow, it was distasteful, and it was a lot of fun."

5   Zuckerberg was lucky that he was not expelled. Harvard did charge him with violating the students' privacy and the school's security and copyrights. Zuckerberg

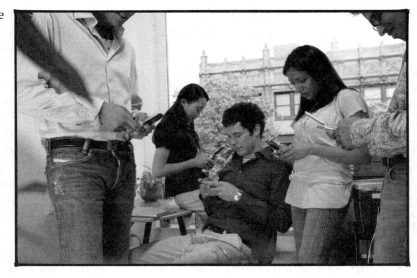

Facebook has become a routine in many people's lives, partly because it can be accessed from almost anywhere.

94

apologized to his fellow students on his blog, but he also left himself an escape clause: "Oh well," he wrote, "someone had to do it eventually." In this qualifying statement, Zuckerberg revealed a naked truth: Facemash fascinated, shocked, and delighted university students. Zuckerberg had uncovered a long-time secret pleasure, and delivered it in a trendy package of 21st-century technology. The buzz it created meant that the students really wanted more.

6   Meanwhile, Harvard promised to launch its own official face book Web site for students. Again Zuckerberg grew impatient with the school's promise, and he decided to do it himself, this time without hacking into the school's records or invading students' privacy. "I think it's kind of silly that it would take the university a couple of years to get around to it," he told *The Harvard Crimson*. "I can do it better than they can, and I can do it in a week."

7   Zuckerberg did spend about a week. He worked out computer codes with co-founders Dustin Moskovitz, Chris Hughes, and Eduardo Saverin. Then, on February 4, 2004, he launched a social networking Web site called "thefacebook.com." The site encouraged students to upload their own pictures and whatever personal and academic information they chose to share. Several dozen people registered at first, and within 24 hours between 1200 and 1500 Harvard students had joined. Zuckerberg said that the most important advantage of

the site was that it allowed students to search for other students with the same classes so that they could form study groups. Facebook, as it became known, created a strong sense of community among Harvard students. They logged on to find out what other students thought about their classes and their professors. They chatted to find out which dormitories were the cleanest or safest, who had used books to sell, and where the fun was and who was going.

8   About a month later, Zuckerberg expanded the registration to allow students at Yale, Stanford, and Columbia universities to join Facebook too. Then all Ivy League schools and other Boston-area colleges could join, and gradually most universities in Canada and the United States were allowed. In June, Zuckerberg dropped out of Harvard and moved his operation to Palo Alto, California. Facebook became available to high school students in 2005. A year later, it expanded to include anyone aged 13 or older with a valid e-mail address.

9   Zuckerberg has weathered a number of controversies related to the popularity of his social network site in recent years. Three Harvard students have sued him, claiming that he stole their idea for a social network Web site. There also has been concern that Facebook's social networking features and settings violate privacy rights. These complaints were started by users who accidentally shared personal information without knowing it. Zuckerberg added

privacy controls to try and balance these complaints, and then found he had to make even more adjustments when users grumbled that the controls were too complicated. In 2010 Zuckerberg again was pressured to address the privacy problem. He responded by providing new and easier controls to let people know what they were sharing online and with whom.

10   By July 2010 Facebook had more than 500 million active users, with more and more people signing up every day. Most people have an opinion about social media, and they like to debate its benefits and faults. However, almost all will agree that Mark Zuckerberg's Facebook has greatly changed the way people of all ages share information and stay in touch. ✳

If you have been timed while reading this article, enter your reading time below. Then turn to the Words-per-Minute Table on page 101 and look up your reading speed (words per minute). Enter your reading speed on the graph on page 102.

Reading Time: Lesson 10

_____ : _____
Minutes   Seconds

A | Finding the Main Idea

One statement below expresses the main idea of the article. One statement is too general, or too broad. The other statement explains only part of the article; it is too narrow. Label the statements using the following key:

M—Main Idea   **B—Too Broad**   **N—Too Narrow**

_____ 1. Facebook is an international sensation and continues to grow.

_____ 2. Computer wizard Mark Zuckerberg created a wildly popular social networking Web site called Facebook, in which users can connect to each other online.

_____ 3. Many people are concerned that Facebook violates the user's need for privacy.

_____ Score 15 points for a correct M answer.

_____ Score 5 points for each correct B or N answer.

_____ **Total Score**: Finding the Main Idea

B | Recalling Facts

How well do you remember the facts in the article? Put an X in the box next to the answer that correctly completes each statement about the article.

1. Mark Zuckerberg wrote his first computer program
    ☐ a. in sixth grade.
    ☐ b. in high school.
    ☐ c. at Harvard University.

2. Zuckerberg paired photos of students on his Web site called
    ☐ a. Synapse.
    ☐ b. Facemash.
    ☐ c. Facebook.

3. Zuckerberg and his co-founders created Facebook
    ☐ a. over a period of about one month.
    ☐ b. in just one day.
    ☐ c. in about a week.

4. After Zuckerberg dropped out of college, he moved his operation to
    ☐ a. Palo Alto, California.
    ☐ b. Phoenix, Arizona.
    ☐ c. Boston, Massachusetts.

5. By July 2010 there were at least
    ☐ a. one billion Facebook users.
    ☐ b. 500 million Facebook users.
    ☐ c. 5 billion Facebook users.

Score 5 points for each correct answer.

_____ **Total Score**: Recalling Facts

C | Making Inferences

When you combine your own experiences and information from a text to draw a conclusion that is not directly stated in that text, you are making an inference. Below are five statements that may or may not be inferences based on information in the article. Label the statements using the following key:

C—Correct Inference   **F—Faulty Inference**

_____ 1. Zuckerberg probably knew more about computers than most of his elementary school teachers knew.

_____ 2. Zuckerberg's only goal in creating his computer programs was to get rich.

_____ 3. Quite often, college ID photos are not flattering.

_____ 4. Zuckerberg didn't know what kind of social networking site Harvard students wanted.

_____ 5. Facebook is popular only with students and young people.

Score 5 points for each correct answer.

_____ **Total Score**: Making Inferences

D | Using Words Precisely

Each numbered sentence below contains an underlined word or phrase from the article. Following the sentence are three definitions. One definition is closest to the meaning of the underlined word. One definition is opposite or nearly opposite. Label those two definitions using the following key. Do not label the remaining definition.

C—Closest   **O—Opposite or Nearly Opposite**

1. "They kept on saying that there were all these reasons why they couldn't <u>aggregate</u> this information," he said.

    _____ a. scatter

    _____ b. gather together

    _____ c. identify

2. In just four hours, the site went <u>viral</u>, with 450 visitors and 22,000 photo views.

    _____ a. so popular that it seemed out of control

    _____ b. entirely unnoticed

    _____ c. off-track

3. "It was <u>callow</u>, it was distasteful, and it was a lot of fun."

    _____ a. exciting, daring

    _____ b. immature, youthful

    _____ c. sophisticated

4. In one <u>qualifying</u> statement, Zuckerberg revealed a naked truth.

    _____ a. making less harsh or offensive

    _____ b. mocking or laughing at

    _____ c. challenging

5. Zuckerberg has weathered a number of <u>controversies</u> related to the popularity of his social network site in recent years.

_____ a. discussions in which all participants agree

_____ b. remarkable experiences

_____ c. disputes or arguments

_____ Score 3 points for each correct C answer.

_____ Score 2 points for each correct O answer.

_____ **Total Score**: Using Words Precisely

Enter the four total scores in the spaces below, and add them together to find your Reading Comprehension Score. Then record your score on the graph on page 103.

Score	Question Type	Lesson 10
_____	Finding the Main Idea	
_____	Recalling Facts	
_____	Making Inferences	
_____	Using Words Precisely	
_____	**Reading Comprehension Score**	

Author's Approach

Put an X in the box next to the correct answer.

1. The author uses the first sentence of the article to

☐ a. raise the reader's curiosity about what Mark Zuckerberg did to make people angry.

☐ b. compare Mark Zuckerberg with other students.

☐ c. defend Mark Zuckerberg against criticism.

2. Choose the statement below that is the weakest argument for using Facebook.

☐ a. It connects users so they can share information.

☐ b. It is fun and interesting.

☐ c. It can easily reveal more about its users than was intended.

3. The author probably wrote this article in order to

☐ a. inform the reader about what Facebook offers.

☐ b. persuade the reader to join Facebook.

☐ c. describe how one person changed the way people communicate.

4. Read and think about the following statement from the article: "Zuckerberg apologized to his fellow students on his blog but also left himself an escape clause: 'Oh well,' he wrote, 'someone had to do it eventually.'" You can conclude that the author wants the reader to think that

☐ a. Zuckerberg was extremely embarrassed and sorry.

☐ b. Zuckerberg didn't seem too sorry for what he did.

☐ c. Zuckerberg was sure that his idea had been a bad one.

_____ Number of correct answers

Record your personal assessment of your work on the Critical Thinking Chart on page 104.

CRITICAL THINKING

Summarizing and Paraphrasing

Put an X in the box next to the correct answer for the questions 1 and 2. Follow the directions provided for question 3.

1. Choose the best one-sentence paraphrase for the following sentence from the article: "Facebook, as it became known, created a strong sense of community among Harvard students."

   ☐ a. Facebook revealed that Harvard students were a close-knit group.

   ☐ b. Facebook pulled Harvard students together.

   ☐ c. Facebook reminded Harvard students about their responsibilities to the community.

2. Read the statement about the article below. Then read the paraphrase of that statement. Choose the reason that best tells why the paraphrase does not say the same thing as the statement.

   Statement: The site made it possible for students to upload their own pictures and to share personal information.

   Paraphrase: Using the site, students were able to share information about themselves.

   ☐ a. Paraphrase says too much.

   ☐ b. Paraphrase doesn't say enough.

   ☐ c. Paraphrase doesn't agree with the statement.

3. Look for the important ideas and events in paragraphs 6 and 7. Summarize those paragraphs in one or two sentences.

   _____

   _____

   _____

   _____

_____ Number of correct answers

Record your personal assessment of your work on the Critical Thinking Chart on page 104.

Critical Thinking

Follow the directions provided for questions 1 and 5. Put an X next to the correct answer for the other questions.

1. For each statement below, write O if it expresses an opinion or write F if it expresses a fact.

   _____ a. "A lot of them complained about having their images displayed without their knowledge or consent."

   _____ b. "It was during his sophomore year at Harvard that Zuckerberg's life got really interesting."

   _____ c. "I think it's kind of silly that it would take the university a couple of years to get around to it," he told *The Harvard Crimson*.

2. From what the article told about Mark Zuckerberg, you can predict that

   ☐ a. he will apologize for creating Facebook.

   ☐ b. he will expand the possibilities of social networking.

   ☐ c. he will remove privacy controls from Facebook.

3. What was the effect of Zuckerman's creating the Web site Facemash?

   ☐ a. Harvard took over Zuckerman's Internet connection.

   ☐ b. Zuckerman made a great deal of money.

   ☐ c. Students were easily able to connect with their fellow students.

4. How is Mark Zuckerberg an example of the theme of *Visionaries*?

   ☐ a. Zuckerberg recognized a social need and filled it.

   ☐ b. Zuckerberg is willing to risk failure in order to succeed.

   ☐ c. Zuckerberg has excellent computer skills.

CRITICAL THINKING

5. In which paragraph did you find your information or details to answer question 3?

    _____

> _____ Number of correct answers
>
> Record your personal assessment of your work on the Critical Thinking Chart on page 104.

Personal Response

How do you think Mark Zuckerberg felt after he turned down the money and job offers that followed the success of his Synapse program?

_____

_____

_____

_____

_____

_____

_____

Self-Assessment

The part I found most difficult about the article was

_____

_____

_____

_____

_____

_____

I found this difficult because

_____

_____

_____

_____

_____

_____

_____

CRITICAL THINKING

Compare and Contrast

Think about the articles you have read in Unit Two. Choose three articles that described events that were most interesting to you. Write the titles of the articles in the first column of the chart below. Use information you learned from the articles to fill in the empty boxes in the chart.

Title	What point was the visionary trying to make by his or her actions?	What advice would you have given to this visionary?	What are the most important effects of the visionary's work?

This visionary's achievement is the most memorable to me: _____

_____

_____

_____.

Words-per-Minute Table

Unit Two

Directions If you were timed while reading an article, refer to the Reading Time you recorded in the box at the end of the article. Use this words-per-minute table to determine your reading speed for that article. Then plot your reading speed on the graph on page 102.

Lesson	6	7	8	9	10	
No. of Words	1208	1116	1202	1191	1150	Seconds
1:30	805	744	801	794	767	90
1:40	725	670	721	715	690	100
1:50	659	609	656	650	627	110
2:00	604	558	601	596	575	120
2:10	558	515	555	550	531	130
2:20	518	478	515	510	493	140
2:30	483	446	481	476	460	150
2:40	453	419	451	447	431	160
2:50	426	394	424	420	406	170
3:00	403	372	401	397	383	180
3:10	381	352	380	376	363	190
3:20	362	335	361	357	345	200
3:30	345	319	343	340	329	210
3:40	329	304	328	325	314	220
3:50	315	291	314	311	300	230
4:00	302	279	301	298	288	240
4:10	290	268	288	286	276	250
4:20	279	258	277	275	265	260
4:30	268	248	267	265	256	270
4:40	259	239	258	255	246	280
4:50	250	231	249	246	238	290
5:00	242	223	240	238	230	300
5:10	234	216	233	231	223	310
5:20	227	209	225	223	216	320
5:30	220	203	219	217	209	330
5:40	213	197	212	210	203	340
5:50	207	191	206	204	197	350
6:00	201	186	200	199	192	360
6:10	196	181	195	193	186	370
6:20	191	176	190	188	182	380
6:30	186	172	185	183	177	390
6:40	181	167	180	179	173	400
6:50	177	163	176	174	168	410
7:00	173	159	172	170	164	420
7:10	169	156	168	166	160	430
7:20	165	152	164	162	157	440
7:30	161	149	160	159	153	450
7:40	158	146	157	155	150	460
7:50	154	142	153	152	147	470
8:00	151	140	150	149	144	480

Minutes and Seconds

Plotting Your Progress: Reading Speed

Unit Two

Directions If you were timed while reading an article, write your words-per-minute rate for that article in the box under the number of the lesson. Then plot your reading speed on the graph by putting a small X on the line directly above the number of the lesson, across from the number of words per minute you read. As you mark your speed for each lesson, graph your progress by drawing a line to connect the Xs.

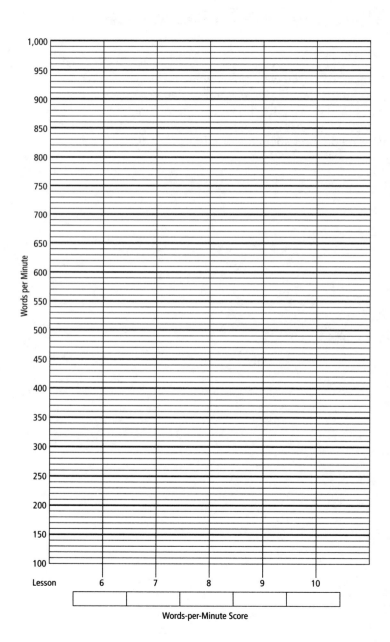

Plotting Your Progress: Reading Comprehension

Unit Two

Directions Write your Reading Comprehension score for each lesson in the box under the number of the lesson. Then plot your score on the graph by putting a small X on the line directly above the number of the lesson and across from the score you earned. As you mark your score for each lesson, graph your progress by drawing a line to connect the Xs.

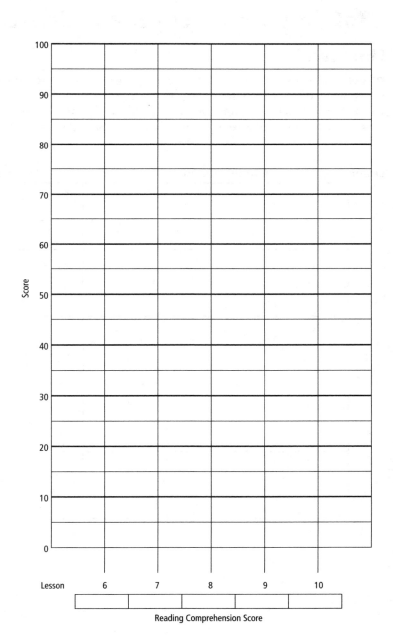

Plotting Your Progress: Critical Thinking

Unit Two

Directions Work with your teacher to evaluate your responses to the Critical Thinking questions for each lesson. Then fill in the appropriate spaces in the chart below. For each lesson and each type of Critical Thinking question, do the following: Mark a minus sign (–) in the box to indicate areas in which you feel you could improve. Mark a plus sign (+) to indicate areas in which you feel you did well. Mark a minus-slash-plus sign (–/+) to indicate areas in which you had mixed success. Then write any comments you have about your performance, including ideas for improvement.

Lesson	Author's Approach	Summarizing and Paraphrasing	Critical Thinking
6			
7			
8			
9			
10			

Unit Three

Caught on the Web

Shannen Rossmiller hunts terrorists by pretending to be one of them.

On September 3, 2004, a man calling himself Amir Abdul Rashid was court-martialed and sentenced to five concurrent life terms in prison. He was convicted of trying to supply a foreign terrorist network with information about American troops—their strength and tactics—and provide methods for killing American soldiers. The traitor, whose real name was Ryan Anderson, was a United States citizen and a National Guardsman who was about to be sent to fight in Iraq. Three years earlier, Anderson had converted to Islam. He had decided that he was "on the wrong side" of the conflict with terrorists and vowed to do whatever he could to hurt the United States.

2   How was Anderson's plot against the United States discovered? Was he tracked by a government intelligence agency, or did the military police discover Anderson's intentions? No, in fact, Anderson was caught by a private citizen named Shannen Rossmiller—a mother of three from a small town in Montana. Rossmiller, who is a municipal judge by day, trapped Anderson on the Internet by posing as a terrorist sympathizer.

3   Rossmiller began her strategy right after the terrorist attacks of September 11, 2001, on the World Trade Center in New York City and the Pentagon in Washington, D.C.

At the time, she was confined to her bed at home while she recovered from a broken pelvis she suffered in a fall. Those long hours of very little movement gave Rossmiller plenty of time to watch the television coverage and analysis of the terrorist attacks. "I wondered how it could happen," she wrote in 2007 in the *Middle East Quarterly*. "What kind of people could carry out such an atrocity and why?" Her anger and curiosity drove her to find out. "I saw a news report about how the terrorists and their sympathizers communicated on Web sites and Internet message boards." It said the U.S. government agencies had little or no ability to monitor these Internet communications. The report described some of these communications and also provided an Internet address that terrorists had used. Rossmiller, sufficiently stirred up, typed in the URL and logged on to the site.

4   Rossmiller was not qualified and had no experience in collecting intelligence, but after several visits to the Web site she saw enough to know that it was for real. Once Rossmiller knew where to find the terrorist forums and how to infiltrate them, she wanted to take the next step. Since she couldn't read a word of Arabic, there was no way for her to understand exactly what the extremists were saying. Rossmiller solved that by signing up for two intensive online courses in Arabic. She soon learned enough of the language to understand some of the information being passed back and forth. She also began to figure out which individuals were the most radical players.

As her knowledge and language skills improved, she started posting some of her own supportive messages in order to lure terrorists to communicate with her. After a while, she found an Arabic language translator through an online translation service who helped her construct accurate messages. She also added software to disguise her Montana computer address so she could appear to be online from Pakistan or some other place. With these tools and her improving language skills, Rossmiller began sending disguised messages and receiving responses from America's terrorist enemies.

5   It was at this point, in March of 2002, that Rossmiller created her first terrorist cover identity—that of a Middle Eastern arms dealer. She was so convincing that a Pakistani man offered to sell her stolen U.S. Stinger missiles to be used against U.S. troops in Afghanistan. She demanded that the man provide her with the identification numbers on the missiles to confirm that he actually had them. When he did so, Rossmiller

passed the information on to a national security agency, which later confirmed that the numbers matched U.S. Stinger missiles that had been missing. With this success, Rossmiller was encouraged to go deeper into the online world of terrorists.

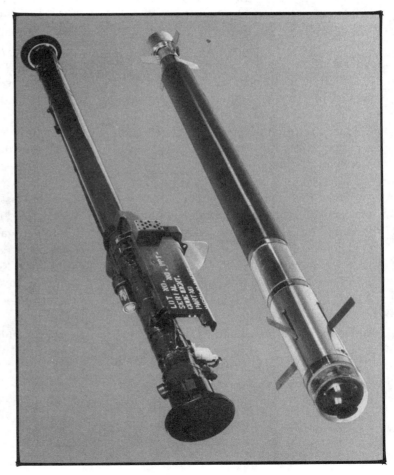

Shoulder-fired Stinger missiles were among the goods that Rossmiller pretended she could buy from terrorists.

6   In October 2003, while surfing various terrorist Web sites, she came across a message in English posted by a man calling himself Amir Abdul Rashid. The man wrote that he was ready to "take things to the next level in the fight against our enemy." Rossmiller found it strange that someone would post a message in English on an Arabic Web site. She traced his computer IP address back to the state of Washington. After a little while, it became clear to Rossmiller that the man was a member of the U.S. military. Rossmiller pretended to be a radical from Algeria with close ties to the Al-Qaeda terrorist network, and she offered her support. Rashid—whose original name was Ryan Anderson—wrote back. The two exchanged a total of 30 e-mails in English. Anderson revealed to Rossmiller that he was a member of a tank battalion about to be sent to Iraq. He told her about certain weaknesses of the tanks and divulged U.S. troop locations in Iraq. What Anderson didn't know was that Rossmiller was sharing all of this critical information with U.S. security. On February 12, 2004, Ryan Anderson was arrested and turned over to the U.S. military for trial.

7   Rossmiller wanted very much to remain unknown and continue working out of her home late into the night. But after the trial of Ryan Anderson, in which she was a key witness for the prosecution, her undercover role as well as her identity became part of the public court record. She began receiving death threats, and on December 5, 2004, someone stole her car out of the family garage. The police later found it wrecked and riddled with bullet holes. After that, the government provided her with a permanent personal security team.

8   Rossmiller continued her work over the next few years, trapping and exposing individuals who were planning to carry out terrorist activities. She assumed about 30 fictitious identities and helped to provide information in more than 200 international spy and terrorism cases. In one case, she exposed an American drifter named Michael Curtis Reynolds, who planned to blow up Alaskan oil pipelines because he was opposed to the Iraq war. Once again, Rossmiller was called to testify in open court. Because much of the prosecution's case against Reynolds rested on her testimony, Rossmiller felt intense stress and pressure over the case. She says, "I was vomiting blood before I had to testify in court against Reynolds. I developed kidney stones and a bleeding ulcer. It takes you down. I thought it was going to be the end of me."

9   Reynolds ultimately was convicted and sentenced to 30 years in prison, but Rossmiller had enough, and she decided it was time to give up her one-person counterterrorism operation. In 2009 she met with defense companies and intelligence agencies, who arranged to provide money and support for her to teach others how to track and trap terrorists.

10   On September 11, 2001, Rossmiller was not thinking about herself or her broken pelvis. Like many others, she was angry and wanted to put her anger to positive use. So Rossmiller applied her curiosity, will, and intelligence toward a spark of an idea that grew and shed light on the shadowy world of terrorism. ✳

If you have been timed while reading this article, enter your reading time below. Then turn to the Words-per-Minute Table on page 147 and look up your reading speed (words per minute). Enter your reading speed on the graph on page 148.

Reading Time: Lesson 11

_____ : _____
Minutes   *Seconds*

A Finding the Main Idea

One statement below expresses the main idea of the article. One statement is too general, or too broad. The other statement explains only part of the article; it is too narrow. Label the statements using the following key:

M—Main Idea   **B—Too Broad**   **N—Too Narrow**

_____ 1. After exchanging 30 e-mails with a suspected terrorist, Shannen Rossmiller shared what she knew with government security, and the terrorist was arrested.

_____ 2. By infiltrating terrorist Web sites and posing as a terrorist sympathizer, Shannen Rossmiller was able to lure and catch terrorists.

_____ 3. Shannen Rossmiller proved that the Internet can be an effective weapon in the fight against terrorism.

_____ Score 15 points for a correct M answer.

_____ Score 5 points for each correct B or N answer.

_____ **Total Score**: Finding the Main Idea

B Recalling Facts

How well do you remember the facts in the article? Put an X in the box next to the answer that correctly completes each statement about the article.

1. On September 11, 2001, Shannen Rossmiller was a
    - ☐ a. language translator.
    - ☐ b. municipal judge.
    - ☐ c. member of U.S. national security.

2. Rossmiller's first step in fighting terrorism was to
    - ☐ a. log on to suspected terrorist Web sites.
    - ☐ b. learn to read and write Arabic.
    - ☐ c. ask the government what she could do as a private citizen.

3. The terrorist known as Amir Abdul Rashid was actually
    - ☐ a. a member of the U.S. military.
    - ☐ b. an Islamist arms dealer.
    - ☐ c. an unemployed drifter.

4. The government provided security to Rossmiller after
    - ☐ a. she became sick before a tense trial.
    - ☐ b. her car was stolen and then found riddled with bullets.
    - ☐ c. met with defense companies and intelligence agencies.

5. Terrorist Michael Curtis Reynolds's plan was to
    - ☐ a. fly a plane into the World Trade Center.
    - ☐ b. leak information about American troop strength.
    - ☐ c. blow up oil pipelines.

Score 5 points for each correct answer.

_____ **Total Score**: Recalling Facts

C Making Inferences

When you combine your own experiences and information from a text to draw a conclusion that is not directly stated in that text, you are making an inference. Below are five statements that may or may not be inferences based on information in the article. Label the statements using the following key:

C—Correct Inference   **F—Faulty Inference**

_____ 1. Rossmiller would not have cared as deeply about the events of 9/11 had she had not been injured.

_____ 2. Rossmiller believed that her car was stolen and damaged by people who were against her counterterrorism activities.

_____ 3. It is relatively easy to successfully pretend to be someone other than yourself online.

_____ 4. Rossmiller could have brought the terrorists to justice on her own, without working with any government agency.

_____ 5. Only people from outside the United States are involved in anti-American terrorist activities.

Score 5 points for each correct answer.

_____ **Total Score**: Making Inferences

D Using Words Precisely

Each numbered sentence below contains an underlined word or phrase from the article. Following the sentence are three definitions. One definition is closest to the meaning of the underlined word. One definition is opposite or nearly opposite. Label those two definitions using the following key. Do not label the remaining definition.

C—Closest   **O—Opposite or Nearly Opposite**

1. Rossmiller, who is a municipal judge by day, trapped Anderson on the Internet by posing as a terrorist <u>sympathizer</u>.

   _____ a. someone who opposes

   _____ b. someone who supports

   _____ c. someone who learns about

2. Once Rossmiller knew where to find the terrorist forums and how to <u>infiltrate</u> them, she wanted to take the next step.

   _____ a. break into

   _____ b. recognize

   _____ c. run away from

3. She also began to figure out which individuals were the most <u>radical</u> players.

   _____ a. extreme

   _____ b. moderate, thoughtful

   _____ c. intelligent

4. He told her about certain weaknesses of the tanks and <u>divulged</u> U.S. troop locations in Iraq.

   _____ a. concealed

   _____ b. attacked

   _____ c. revealed

5. She assumed about 30 <u>fictitious</u> identities and helped to provide information in more than 200 international spy and terrorism cases.

_____ a. formal

_____ b. factual

_____ c. imagined or invented

_____ Score 3 points for each correct C answer.

_____ Score 2 points for each correct O answer.

_____ **Total Score**: Using Words Precisely

Enter the four total scores in the spaces below, and add them together to find your Reading Comprehension Score. Then record your score on the graph on page 149.

Score	Question Type	Lesson 11
_____	Finding the Main Idea	
_____	Recalling Facts	
_____	Making Inferences	
_____	Using Words Precisely	
_____	**Reading Comprehension Score**	

Author's Approach

Put an X in the box next to the correct answer.

1. From the statements below, choose the ones that you believe the author would agree with.

☐ a. Rossmiller showed persistence, cleverness, and courage in her fight against terrorism.

☐ b. Terrorists are extremely cautious on the Internet.

☐ c. Rossmiller made valuable contributions to the United States.

2. The author tells this story mainly by

☐ a. retelling personal experiences.

☐ b. comparing different topics.

☐ c. describing events in the order they happened.

3. Which of the following statements from the article best describes how Rossmiller fought terrorism?

☐ a. "At the time, she was confined to her bed at home while she recovered from a broken pelvis she suffered in a fall."

☐ b. "With these tools and her improving language skills, Rossmiller began sending disguised messages and receiving responses from America's terrorist enemies."

☐ c. "No, in fact, Anderson was caught by a private citizen named Shannen Rossmiller—a mother of three from a small town in Montana."

4. The author probably wrote this article to

☐ a. encourage readers to trap terrorists on the Internet.

☐ b. raise awareness about terrorism.

☐ c. tell about one person's single-handed response to terrorism.

_____ Number of correct answers

Record your personal assessment of your work on the Critical Thinking Chart on page 150.

CRITICAL THINKING

Summarizing and Paraphrasing

Put an X in the box next to the correct answer for question 1. Follow the directions provided for question 2.

1. Choose the best one-sentence paraphrase for the following sentence from the article: "Rossmiller found it strange that someone would post a message in English on an Arabic Web site."

   ☐ a. Although the message was in English, someone had posted it on an Arabic Web site.

   ☐ b. Rossmiller's message, strangely enough, was in Arabic, even though the Web site was in English.

   ☐ c. It seemed unusual to Rossmiller that an English message had been posted on an Arabic Web site.

2. Complete the following one-sentence summary of the article using the lettered phrases from the phrase bank below. Write the letters on the lines.

Phrase Bank:

a. Rossmiller's decision to retire and to teach others the tactics she had learned

b. Rossmiller's successes in trapping terrorists

c. Rossmiller's reaction to the September 11 attacks

The article "Caught on the Web" begins with _____, goes on to describe _____, and ends with _____.

_____ Number of correct answers

Record your personal assessment of your work on the Critical Thinking Chart on page 150.

Critical Thinking

Put an X in the box next to the correct answer for questions 1, 3, and 4. Follow the directions provided for the other questions.

1. Judging by the events in the article, you can predict that the following might happen next:

   ☐ a. Terrorists will stop communicating over the Internet.

   ☐ b. Intelligence agencies will trap more terrorists using Rossmiller's tactics.

   ☐ c. Rossmiller will decide to resume her Internet counterterrorism.

2. Think about cause-effect relationships in the article. Fill in the blanks in the cause-effect chart, drawing from the letters below.

Cause	Effect
Rossmiller broke her pelvis.	_____
_____	He planned to blow up pipelines.
Rossmiller testified at Anderson's trial.	_____

   a. Reynolds was against the war in Iraq.

   b. She began to get death threats.

   c. She was home watching TV on September 11, 2001.

3. Of the following theme categories, which would this story fit into?

   ☐ a. Don't complain. Just work harder.

   ☐ b. One should learn to forgive and forget.

   ☐ c. Don't try to walk before you can crawl.

4. From the information in paragraph 4, you can conclude that

☐ a. some of what Rossmiller read on the terrorist Web sites must have been written in English.

☐ b. all of the terrorist communications Rossmiller read on the Web sites were in Arabic.

☐ c. to log on to terrorist Web sites, you had to know how to read and write Arabic.

5. Which paragraphs provide evidence that supports your answer to question 2?

_____

_____ Number of correct answers

Record your personal assessment of your work on the Critical Thinking Chart on page 150.

Personal Response

What details surprised or interested you the most in this article?

_____

_____

_____

_____

Self-Assessment

From reading this article, I have learned

_____

_____

_____

_____

_____

_____

_____

_____

_____

CRITICAL THINKING

Building the Panama Canal

The Panama Canal was carved through more than 50 miles of hilly terrain.

Five hundred years ago, when Spanish explorers came to the New World, they were thrilled to discover gold, silver, and other riches there. But these treasures were concentrated along the west coast of South America, in what today are the countries of Ecuador and Peru. A cursory glance at a world map reveals the problem of getting all that wealth back to Spain. There simply was no efficient route from the west coast of South America to Europe. No route, that is, unless a canal could be built that cut through the narrow strip of land connecting North and South America.

2   By 1529 Spanish engineers had drawn up such a plan, and in the late 1800s, a French engineer named Ferdinand Marie de Lesseps gave it new life. De Lesseps had managed the construction of Egypt's Suez Canal, which was completed in 1869. Seeking more success, de Lesseps, in 1875, announced his intention to connect the Atlantic and Pacific oceans by carving a canal through the strip of land now called the Isthmus of Panama.

3   De Lesseps's vision for the canal and the willingness of the French government to build it, however, were not in harmony. He promoted his idea by promising that the project would be inexpensive, but rumors swirled that he had to bribe officials to vote for it. What's more, de Lesseps thought he could build a sea-level canal like the one he had constructed in Egypt. A sea-level canal is basically a deep trench that connects two large bodies of water. Cutting such a deep channel through level sand in the low desert region of Egypt was comparatively easy and cheap. But Panama's landscape was not the same as Egypt's. Panama is mountainous, so a staggering amount of soil, clay, and rock would have to be removed. Streams would need to be diverted also, and a tidal basin constructed to collect water from the rivers when they overflowed. To be successful, de Lesseps would have to change a mountain ridge into a valley, with a canal deep and wide enough for large ships to pass.

4   From the beginning, the project seemed to get off on the wrong foot. January 1, 1880, was the day of the ground-breaking ceremony, where de Lesseps was to place his pick into the ground to symbolize the beginning of construction. His family and important officials took a boat to the place along the Rio Grande River where the ceremony was to be held. But the boat was stopped two or three miles from the shore because the tide began to go out. Rather than call off the ceremony, someone collected a small amount of Panamanian soil in a box and placed it on the deck. De Lesseps stuck his ceremonial pick into the box as the party guests cheered. It was a strange and funny celebration, but de Lesseps's problems had only just begun.

5   In the years that followed, the engineers found out that the excavating machines they had brought from France did a poor job of moving large boulders. They ended up having to break them up with hand tools.

President Theodore Roosevelt handles the controls of a steam shovel during a visit to the Panama Canal around 1906.

To make matters worse, mosquitoes that carried deadly diseases such as yellow fever and malaria swarmed the French workers, who had no defense against tropical diseases. More than 20,000 of them died, and many more were made weak by illness, overwork, and poor living conditions. By 1889 the company that de Lesseps had formed to build the canal was bankrupt, and work ceased with only about two-fifths of the canal completed. The French government was not pleased with the failure and the waste. De Lesseps was prosecuted by the French court and convicted of fraud, though charges against him were later dropped.

6   Another French company took over, but by 1899, the French were ready to admit defeat. The tropical heat, disease, and rocky terrain seemed to turn the vision of a Panama Canal into a fading shadow. The United States, in the meantime, had been watching with interest and making its own plans. And why not? A canal would benefit the United States most of all. At that time most long-haul trade and travel was done by ships. A U.S.-built water passage through Panama would shorten the journey from New York City to San Francisco by 18,000 miles!

7   In 1904 the United States arranged for control of a 10-mile wide strip of land known as the Panama Canal Zone. After a year, however, the Americans seemed stuck in the same rut the French had fallen into. The U.S. project gained traction in 1905 when President Theodore Roosevelt appointed John F. Stevens as the chief engineer. Stevens didn't agree with de Lesseps's vision of a canal at sea level; he imagined a canal that adjusted to the hills and valleys of Panama.

8   Stevens's engineers thought of a plan to build canal locks rather than dig a long trench. In a lock system, a ship would sail into a narrow channel, or lock, which would fill up with water, causing the ship to rise to a higher level. Then the lock would open and the ship would proceed into the next lock. This next lock would move the ship up to the following lock, eventually raising the ship about 85 feet above sea level. The ship would then sail across an artificial lake to the remaining locks, where it would gradually be lowered back down until it reached the ocean. This lock system would reduce the amount of digging that was required. If a double set of locks was built side by side, ships could pass through the canal in both directions at the same time.

9   Stevens's idea to use locks was a brilliant revision of de Lesseps's plan. Still, Stevens knew that serious problems remained. The French had never figured out how to remove the soil from the areas they excavated. Stevens solved this by building a railroad in the Canal Zone that carried away 200 trainloads of dirt each day. Next, he organized an intense campaign to eradicate the mosquitoes that were spreading malaria and yellow fever. He accomplished this by spraying all standing or slow-moving bodies of water with a combination of oil and insecticide. He also built better housing for the 25,000 workers. Sanitation was enforced, and medical staff and supplies were brought into the Canal Zone. Once the area was under control, the real work of building the canal could begin. However, Stevens knew the work that remained—the level of engineering required to design the locks—was beyond his abilities. In early 1907, he resigned, and President Roosevelt appointed Army Lieutenant George Goethals as the new chief engineer of the canal project. Goethals proved to be a good choice. For the next seven years, he brought military-style pace and discipline to the construction of 65-foot high locks and three dams, including the massive Gatun Dam.

10   It took the combined talents and determination of visionaries Ferdinand de Lesseps, John Stevens, and George Goethals to bring the mammoth project to completion. The 51-mile Panama Canal was finally opened to shipping in August 1914, and it has been considered one of the "Seven Wonders of the Modern World" ever since. ✷

If you have been timed while reading this article, enter your reading time below. Then turn to the Words-per-Minute Table on page 147 and look up your reading speed (words per minute). Enter your reading speed on the graph on page 148.

Reading Time: Lesson 12

_____ : _____
Minutes   *Seconds*

A Finding the Main Idea

One statement below expresses the main idea of the article. One statement is too general, or too broad. The other statement explains only part of the article; it is too narrow. Label the statements using the following key:

M—Main Idea   **B—Too Broad**   **N—Too Narrow**

_____ 1. Ferdinand Marie de Lesseps envisioned the Panama Canal as a long, deep trench between the Atlantic and Pacific Oceans, but that plan proved to be unworkable.

_____ 2. Building the Panama Canal was accomplished through the vision, daring, and determination shown by engineers Ferdinand Marie de Lesseps, John F. Stevens, and George Goethals.

_____ 3. Building the Panama Canal was a difficult and amazing achievement.

_____ Score 15 points for a correct M answer.

_____ Score 5 points for each correct B or N answer.

_____ **Total Score**: Finding the Main Idea

B Recalling Facts

How well do you remember the facts in the article? Put an X in the box next to the answer that correctly completes each statement about the article.

1. Ferdinand Marie de Lesseps was a
☐ a. French government official.
☐ b. personal friend of U.S. President Theodore Roosevelt.
☐ c. French engineer.

2. De Lesseps successfully managed the building of a canal
☐ a. in France.
☐ b. in Egypt.
☐ c. in Spain.

3. Two major diseases that killed canal workers were
☐ a. smallpox and diphtheria.
☐ b. tuberculosis and bubonic plague.
☐ c. malaria and yellow fever.

4. The Panama Canal reduces the water passage between New York City and San Francisco by
☐ a. 18,000 miles.
☐ b. 5,000 miles.
☐ c. 80,000 miles.

5. The Panama Canal finally opened in
☐ a. 1875.
☐ b. 1914.
☐ c. 1941.

Score 5 points for each correct answer.

_____ **Total Score**: Recalling Facts

C Making Inferences

When you combine your own experiences and information from a text to draw a conclusion that is not directly stated in that text, you are making an inference. Below are five statements that may or may not be inferences based on information in the article. Label the statements using the following key:

C—Correct Inference   **F—Faulty Inference**

_____ 1. De Lesseps's plan for the canal definitely would have worked if the government had not run out of money.

_____ 2. It takes a special person to imagine and execute a project as huge and as difficult as the Panama Canal.

_____ 3. John Stevens probably learned a lot from de Lesseps's mistakes when he made his own plans for building the Panama Canal.

_____ 4. Mosquitoes often breed in still or slow-moving water.

_____ 5. Building the Panama Canal actually turned out to be quite easy and inexpensive after George Goethals took over the project.

Score 5 points for each correct answer.

_____ **Total Score**: Making Inferences

D Using Words Precisely

Each numbered sentence below contains an underlined word or phrase from the article. Following the sentence are three definitions. One definition is closest to the meaning of the underlined word. One definition is opposite or nearly opposite. Label those two definitions using the following key. Do not label the remaining definition.

C—Closest   **O—Opposite or Nearly Opposite**

1. A <u>cursory</u> glance at a world map reveals the problem of getting all that wealth back to Spain.

_____ a. flawed and unacceptable

_____ b. quick and superficial

_____ c. careful and thorough

2. He <u>promoted</u> his idea to the French government by promising that the project would be inexpensive.

_____ a. showed disapproval of

_____ b. explained thoroughly

_____ c. advertised and encouraged interest in

3. Streams would need to be <u>diverted</u>, and a tidal basin constructed to collect water from the rivers when they overflow.

_____ a. changed, rerouted

_____ b. maintained in their current paths

_____ c. purified

4. The French had never figured out how to remove the soil from the areas they <u>excavated</u>.

_____ a. passed by

_____ b. smoothed over

_____ c. dug out

5. Next, he organized an intense campaign to <u>eradicate</u> the mosquitoes that were spreading malaria and yellow fever.

_____ a. eliminate

_____ b. study

_____ c. encourage the growth of

_____ Score 3 points for each correct C answer.

_____ Score 2 points for each correct O answer.

_____ **Total Score**: Using Words Precisely

Enter the four total scores in the spaces below, and add them together to find your Reading Comprehension Score. Then record your score on the graph on page 149.

Score	Question Type	Lesson 12
_____	Finding the Main Idea	
_____	Recalling Facts	
_____	Making Inferences	
_____	Using Words Precisely	
_____	**Reading Comprehension Score**	

Author's Approach

Put an X in the box next to the correct answer.

1. The main purpose of the first two paragraphs is to
   - ☐ a. persuade the reader to visit the Panama Canal.
   - ☐ b. summarize the historical events that led to the building of the Panama Canal.
   - ☐ c. explain why de Lesseps decided to build a sea-level canal.

2. How is the author's purpose for writing the article expressed in paragraph 10?
   - ☐ a. This paragraph stresses that the success of the Panama Canal project was the result of the vision, skill, and determination of its three major engineers.
   - ☐ b. This paragraph states that the Panama Canal finally opened to shipping in 1914.
   - ☐ c. This paragraph states that the Panama Canal has become known as one of the "Seven Wonders of the Modern World."

3. Judging by statements from the article "Building the Panama Canal," you can conclude that the author wants the reader to think that
   - ☐ a. building the Panama Canal was not worth the time, money, and effort that it took.
   - ☐ b. the Suez Canal and the Panama Canal were equally hard to build.
   - ☐ c. de Lesseps was overconfident about his ability to build the Panama Canal.

_____ Number of correct answers

Record your personal assessment of your work on the Critical Thinking Chart on page 150.

CRITICAL THINKING

Summarizing and Paraphrasing

Follow the directions provided for question 1. Put an X in the box next to the correct answer for question 2.

1. Complete the following one-sentence summary of the article using the lettered phrases from the phrase bank below. Write the letters on the lines.

Phrase Bank:

a. why the Panama Canal was needed and early plans for it

b. how the project was finally completed by American engineers John Stevens and George Goethals

c. the efforts of de Lesseps and the reasons why he failed to complete the project

---

The article "Building the Panama Canal" begins with _____, goes on to describe _____, and ends with _____.

2. Choose the sentence that correctly restates the following sentence from the article: "The tropical heat, disease, and rocky terrain seemed to turn the vision of a Panama Canal into a fading shadow."

☐ a. Only some could see that building the Panama Canal would involve battling tropical heat, disease, and rocky terrain.

☐ b. Although the Panama Canal was only a vision, the tropical heat, disease, and rocky terrain were definitely real.

☐ c. After battles with tropical heat, disease, and rocky terrain, it began to seem as if the goal of building a canal in Panama could never be fulfilled.

_____ Number of correct answers

Record your personal assessment of your work on the Critical Thinking Chart on page 150.

Critical Thinking

Put an X in the box next to the correct answer for questions 1 and 3. Follow the directions provided for the other questions.

1. Which of the following statements from the article is an opinion rather than a fact?

☐ a. "Stevens's idea to use locks was a brilliant revision of de Lesseps's plan."

☐ b. "Sanitation was enforced, and medical staff and supplies were brought into the Canal Zone."

☐ c. "The French had never figured out how to remove the soil from the areas they excavated."

2. Using what you know about the French and their efforts to build the Panama Canal and what is told about the Americans and their efforts in the article, name three ways the French were similar to the Americans and three ways the French were different from the Americans. Cite the paragraph number(s) where you found details in the article to support your conclusions.

Similarities

_____

_____

_____

_____

Differences

_____

_____

_____

_____

3. What was the cause of John Stevens's resignation as chief engineer of the Panama Canal?

☐ a. Stevens became ill and was not able to handle the pressure of the project.

☐ b. President Roosevelt lost faith in Stevens's ability to manage the project and demanded his resignation.

☐ c. Stevens felt that he was not capable of designing the needed locks.

4. In which paragraph did you find your information or details to answer question 3?

_____

_____ Number of correct answers

Record your personal assessment of your work on the Critical Thinking Chart on page 150.

Personal Response

What do you think was de Lesseps's biggest mistake?

_____

_____

_____

_____

Self-Assessment

Which concepts or ideas from the article were difficult to understand?

_____

_____

_____

_____

Which were easy to understand?

_____

_____

_____

_____

_____

CRITICAL THINKING

Can Boats Save Bangladesh?

Some Bangladeshi children learn their lessons in a high-tech, solar-powered floating classroom.

He has been called Bangladesh's "Noah"—meaning Noah in the Bible story, who built an ark to save his family and animals from a flood that covered the earth. Abul Hasanat Mohammed Rezwan, a trained architect, isn't rounding up animals two by two, but he may be playing the part of a modern-day Noah just the same. Rezwan believes that another flood is coming—one that will cover his entire native country of Bangladesh. The cause of the deluge, according to scientists and other experts, is climate change. "The catastrophe in Bangladesh has begun," Rezwan says. There have been warnings about the effects of climate change for about a decade, and the International Panel on Climate Change has targeted Bangladesh as a particularly troubled area. There, and in a few other places in the world, the impact of climate change is already having an acute effect on the population. Rezwan heard all of the warnings and saw the devastation. He realized that he could not go on designing buildings "while my country drowns." Instead, he chose to use his training and imagination to put together a survival plan for Bangladesh.

2   Bangladesh, a south Asian nation with about 150 million people, is one of the poorest countries in the world, as well as the most crowded. Climate change has become a living nightmare for this country, which is just barely above sea level. There are about 230 rivers running through Bangladesh, including very large ones such as the Ganges and the Brahmaputra. Historically, Bangladesh's rivers have been its salvation; they irrigate the land with annual floods while renewing the soil's fertility. But in recent years, these floods have become far more extreme. In 2008, after villager Nurjahan Rupbhan's house was washed away by a rising river, she told a reporter, "Until about 10 years ago, the floods came every year and the water would stay for 15 days, and it helped to wet the land. Now the water stays for four months!" The flooding is the result of rising ocean levels combined with torrential monsoon rains and melting Himalayan glaciers. Cyclones, with their heavy rains and powerful waves, routinely wash over Bangladesh and add to the flooding. On June 20, 2008, *The Independent*, a leading British newspaper, ran a special report with this doomsday headline: "Bangladesh is set to disappear under the waves by the end of the century."

3   As the hundreds of rivers in Bangladesh get wider and higher, the amount of dry, useful land shrinks, forcing people to pack their belongings onto rafts, boats, and anything else that floats. To make matters worse, a lot of the land that is left has been stripped of trees and other weather barriers to make room for crops, which makes the land susceptible to erosion. Obviously, this trend cannot go on indefinitely. At some point Bangladeshis will have no land on which to live. Rezwan predicts, "We'll have to live on the water in floating communities, including floating gardens and farms."

Mohammed Rezwan sees the possibility for floating health clinics, gardens, and even floating villages.

4   Rezwan's vision of building floating communities is being applied to solving the most immediate problems facing his country: education and health care. Rezwan remembers the frustration he felt as a child when his school was cancelled because monsoon rains washed away the roads. Now, with the floods lasting months instead of weeks, many students simply drop out of school, especially in the more remote parts of the country. The floods also prevent people in these areas from getting to the hospital or receiving the medicine they need. Many live with no sewage system and no electricity. The lack of clean drinking water means widespread diseases, especially for young children. Says Rezwan, "We decided we must do something to save these people from the slow, creeping disaster that not only threatens human health but also the whole environment."

5   In 1998 Rezwan came up with a first step in relieving the suffering of people in the rural villages affected by sustained flooding. He began a non-profit organization called Shidhulai Swanirvar Sangstha. (Shidhulai is the small village where the charity started, and *Swanirvar Sangstha* means "self-reliance.") Rezwan based his enterprise on the concept that if the people were unable to get to schools and hospitals, he would bring teachers, books, medical staff, and medicines to them. And he would

bring it by boat. "For Bangladesh," he says, "boats are the future."

6   Through his organization, Rezwan has built up a fleet of flat-bottomed, custom-built floating classrooms that make their way through shallow rivers to serve the people who live along the riverbanks. These boats have enough room for 30 children or adults at a time. The shelves in these floating classrooms are lined with more than a thousand books that cover everything from Shakespeare to accounting to science. After the schoolchildren have completed their lessons, the boats change to adult education classrooms. These classes are designed to teach villagers modern farming strategies that they can apply toward controlling soil erosion and producing healthier crops. The boats feature mobile phones and computers with Internet access. DVD players and video projectors are used both for entertainment and educational purposes. Solar panels on roofs generate the electricity needed to run all of this electronic equipment.

7   Rezwan's charity organization also has launched a number of healthcare boats that provide free health services to adults and children. Shidhulai Swanirvar Sangstha distributes solar home systems to bring electricity to people's homes and gives out solar lanterns to aid villagers with their night fishing. All of these services are delivered by about 200 staff members and 2,000 volunteers.

8   By 2009 Rezwan had 54 boats that supported 90,000 families. "I'm immensely pleased with what we're doing," he told a reporter. "With determination and commitment, you can do wonders." However, he quickly admits that he will have to reach at least 20 million people to make a real difference. While some might find this number discouraging, Rezwan merely views it as a challenge. He knows how much good Shidhulai Swanirvar Sangstha can do, and if he ever needs a reminder, he has only to listen to Nurjahan Rupbhan, who says, "I never went to school, and I never saw a doctor in my life. Now my children can do both." ✴

If you have been timed while reading this article, enter your reading time below. Then turn to the Words-per-Minute Table on page 147 and look up your reading speed (words per minute). Enter your reading speed on the graph on page 148.

Reading Time: Lesson 13

_____ : _____
   Minutes   *Seconds*

A Finding the Main Idea

One statement below expresses the main idea of the article. One statement is too general, or too broad. The other statement explains only part of the article; it is too narrow. Label the statements using the following key:

M—Main Idea   **B—Too Broad**   **N—Too Narrow**

_____ 1. Mohammed Rezwan has started a charity organization called Shidhulai Swanirvar Sangstha.

_____ 2. Much of Bangladesh is just barely above sea level, and the more violent weather brought on by climate change is expected to flood the entire country within decades.

_____ 3. In Bangladesh, architect Mohammed Rezwan is using specially equipped boats to bring education and healthcare to people isolated by floods.

_____ Score 15 points for a correct M answer.

_____ Score 5 points for each correct B or N answer.

_____ **Total Score**: Finding the Main Idea

B Recalling Facts

How well do you remember the facts in the article? Put an X in the box next to the answer that correctly completes each statement about the article.

1. The population of Bangladesh is about
☐ a. 20 million.
☐ b. 150 million.
☐ c. 90,000.

2. Brahmaputra is the name of a
☐ a. river in Bangladesh.
☐ b. village in Bangladesh.
☐ c. country near Bangladesh.

3. In Bangladesh, school has to be cancelled when the roads are washed away by
☐ a. melting glaciers.
☐ b. monsoon rains.
☐ c. rising ocean levels.

4. Rezwan started his charity organization in
☐ a. 2009.
☐ b. 2008.
☐ c. 1998.

5. *Swanirvar Sangstha* means
☐ a. "hospital."
☐ b. "charity."
☐ c. "self-reliance."

Score 5 points for each correct answer.

_____ **Total Score**: Recalling Facts

C Making Inferences

When you combine your own experiences and information from a text to draw a conclusion that is not directly stated in that text, you are making an inference. Below are five statements that may or may not be inferences based on information in the article. Label the statements using the following key:

C—Correct Inference   **F—Faulty Inference**

_____ 1. Solar power is the major source of electricity throughout Bangladesh.

_____ 2. Shidhulai Swanirvar Sangstha is the only charity reaching out to the poor people of Bangladesh.

_____ 3. Because of his charity work, Rezwan does not have much time to devote to his career as an architect.

_____ 4. The government of Bangladesh has not been very effective at solving the country's problems.

_____ 5. Because most of the people of Bangladesh are farmers, there are no big cities in the country.

Score 5 points for each correct answer.

_____ **Total Score**: Making Inferences

D Using Words Precisely

Each numbered sentence below contains an underlined word or phrase from the article. Following the sentence are three definitions. One definition is closest to the meaning of the underlined word. One definition is opposite or nearly opposite. Label those two definitions using the following key. Do not label the remaining definition.

C—Closest   **O—Opposite or Nearly Opposite**

1. Climate change is already having an <u>acute</u> effect on the population.

_____ a. critical, severe

_____ b. unimportant, not serious

_____ c. noticeable

2. Rezwan saw the <u>devastation</u> in his country caused by the floods.

_____ a. confusion

_____ b. creation, construction

_____ c. destruction

3. The land has been stripped of trees, which has made it <u>susceptible</u> to erosion

_____ a. damaged, badly used

_____ b. open to change; capable of being affected

_____ c. resistant, protected

4. The people in the villages suffered from the <u>sustained</u> flooding.

_____ a. extended, lengthy

_____ b. sudden, unexpected

_____ c. shortened

5. Modern farming strategies can be applied toward controlling soil <u>erosion</u> and producing healthier crops.

_____ a. firm, solid

_____ b. wearing away

_____ c. replacement

_____ Score 3 points for each correct C answer.

_____ Score 2 points for each correct O answer.

_____ **Total Score**: Using Words Precisely

Enter the four total scores in the spaces below, and add them together to find your Reading Comprehension Score. Then record your score on the graph on page 149.

Score	Question Type	Lesson 13
_____	Finding the Main Idea	
_____	Recalling Facts	
_____	Making Inferences	
_____	Using Words Precisely	
_____	**Reading Comprehension Score**	

Author's Approach

Put an X in the box next to the correct answer.

1. The author uses the first sentence of the article to
   ☐ a. summarize a Bible story for the reader.
   ☐ b. remind the reader of a story about a man who used a boat to save his people.
   ☐ c. give a nickname—Bangladesh's Noah—to the subject of the article.

2. What does the author imply by choosing this quote from Rezwan: "With determination and commitment, you can do wonders"?
   ☐ a. Rezwan does not believe his efforts will accomplish much.
   ☐ b. Rezwan is a hopeful man who is not afraid to take on huge problems.
   ☐ c. Rezwan thinks he can solve the problems of Bangladesh on his own.

3. Considering the statement from the article "Rezwan realized that he could not go on designing buildings 'while my country drowns,'" you can conclude that the author wants the reader to think that
   ☐ a. Rezwan did not feel comfortable working as an architect when his country needed help.
   ☐ b. Rezwan believed his country was totally under water.
   ☐ c. Rezwan thinks he has been wasting his life as an architect.

_____ Number of correct answers

Record your personal assessment of your work on the Critical Thinking Chart on page 150.

Summarizing and Paraphrasing

Put an X in the box next to the correct answer for question 1. Follow the directions provided for question 2.

1. Read the following statement from the article. Then read the paraphrase of that statement. Choose the reason that best tells why the paraphrase does not say the same thing as the statement.

    Statement: The flooding is the result of rising ocean levels combined with torrential monsoon rains and melting Himalayan glaciers.

    Paraphrase: There is flooding because of heavy rains and glaciers melting in the Himalayan mountains.

    ☐ a. Paraphrase says too much.

    ☐ b. Paraphrase doesn't say enough.

    ☐ c. Paraphrase doesn't agree with the statement.

2. Reread paragraph 5 in the article. Below, write a summary of the paragraph in no more than 25 words.

    _____

    _____

    _____

    _____

    _____

    _____

    _____

    _____

    _____

Reread your summary and decide whether it covers the important ideas in the paragraph. Next, decide how to shorten the summary to 15 words or less without leaving out any essential information. Write this summary below.

_____

_____

_____

_____

_____

_____

_____

_____

_____

_____

_____

_____ Number of correct answers

Record your personal assessment of your work on the Critical Thinking Chart on page 150.

Critical Thinking

Put an X in the box next to the correct answer for questions 1, 2, 4, and 5. Follow the directions provided for question 3.

1. Which of the following statements from the article is an opinion rather than a fact?

    ☐ a. "We'll have to live on the water in floating communities, including floating gardens and farms."

    ☐ b. "The International Panel on Climate Change has targeted Bangladesh as a particularly troubled area."

    ☐ c. "There are about 230 rivers running through Bangladesh."

CRITICAL THINKING

2. From what the article told about Rezwan, you can predict that he will

☐ a. concentrate on the healthcare boats only.

☐ b. soon will begin charging the people money for his services.

☐ c. work to expand his organization to bring education and health care to even more people.

3. Choose from the letters below to correctly complete the following statement. Write the letters on the lines.

According to the article, _____, which caused _____, and the effect was that _____.

a. the rivers got wider and wider

b. people packed their belongings onto anything that floats

c. the amount of dry, useful land to shrink

4. How is "Can Boats Save Bangladesh?" an example of the theme of *Visionaries*?

☐ a. Rezwan gave up his job as an architect.

☐ b. Rezwan has not only seen his country's problems, he has thought of a unique approach to solving them.

☐ c. Rezwan's organization offers free services to people.

5. Judging by events in the article, you can conclude that

☐ a. Rezwan is the only person working on a survival plan for Bangladesh.

☐ b. nothing can be done to help Bangladesh's huge problems, even with Rezwan's best efforts.

☐ c. experts around the world are concerned about Bangladesh's flooding problems.

_____ Number of correct answers

Record your personal assessment of your work on the Critical Thinking Chart on page 150.

Personal Response

What was most surprising or interesting to you about this article?

_____

_____

_____

_____

Self-Assessment

I really can't understand how

_____

_____

_____

_____

_____

_____

_____

_____

_____

CRITICAL THINKING

Great Idea, Dr. NakaMats!

People at the 2004 World Genius Convention in Tokyo test the health-benefit claims of Dr. Nakamatsu's Cerebrex chair.

Many highly creative people come up with some sort of custom, routine, or ritual to help themselves focus. To clear their heads and allow the creative juices to flow, they might take a walk in the woods, listen to a favorite piece of music, or sit quietly in a darkened room. But inventor Dr. Yoshiro Nakamatsu has a unique method that definitely is *not* recommended for anyone else. He calls it "creative swimming," and he practices it by diving underwater and staying there for as long as he possibly can. He admits he could black out and maybe even drown by doing this, but he claims the lack of oxygen triggers a flash of creative experience. The rest of us should just to take his word for it.

2   Dr. Nakamatsu says he made his first invention in 1933 at the tender age of five when he created a weighted balancer to help his model air plane fly farther. More inventions soon followed, including an automatic kerosene pump. One of his greatest achievements came as a result of his great love for Beethoven. As a young man of 20, Dr. Nakamatsu loved to listen to the Symphony No. 5 while dreaming up new inventions. Dr. Nakamatsu listened to his favorite Beethoven record so often that the music became distorted with hisses and scratches. "That made me think about how to reproduce sounds without a needle," Dr. Nakamatsu recalls. He set himself the goal of making a better kind of record that would also be smaller, thinner, and less breakable than anything

else on the market. During the next few years, he experimented with a variety of materials that could produce a cleaner sound than vinyl could. In 1952 he received the Japanese patent, or the right to produce, a new device—a "floppy media and drive" that could be read with magnetic and light sensors. This was the first floppy disk design, and it came 20 years before IBM was granted the U.S. patent.

3   Since creating what would become, in effect, the first compact disc, Dr. Nakamatsu has become something of a folk hero in Japan. The people lovingly refer to him as Dr. NakaMats. His prolific career as an inventor also has earned him the unofficial title as "the Edison of Japan." But maybe the order should be reversed; maybe Thomas Edison should be called "the Dr. NakaMats of the United States." After all, Dr. Nakamatsu has more than 3,200 original patents to his credit, and he is always adding more. Edison, by contrast, received only 1,093 patents.

4   Many of Dr. Nakamatsu's inventions are practical gadgets for everyday use, such as the DVD, the digital watch, and the taxicab meter. Others are geared to a unique personal style—for example, the spring-loaded running shoe and the putter that signals with music when

Dr. Nakamatsu tests his Super Pyon Pyon hopping shoes with a young fan in Tokyo.

the golf ball is struck correctly. He has come up with many other good ideas too, but for one reason or another they have never been mass produced, such as an engine that runs on water. He is currently working on plans for a special "next generation" house that is powered completely by cosmic energy. "We receive much power from cosmic sources," Dr. Nakamatsu says.

5   If some of Dr. Nakamatsu's inventions seem quirky, his lifestyle might seem even more so. He sleeps only four hours a night because he believes that sleeping more than six hours out of 24 diminishes brain power. He does allow himself a 20-minute "power nap" during the day, however, but he doesn't just curl up on the couch to snooze. Instead, he uses another one of his special inventions, which he calls the Cerebrex chair. Dr. Nakamatsu explains that the chair improves memory, math skills, and creativity. How does it work? According to the inventor, "Special sound frequencies pulse from the footrest to the headrest, stimulating blood circulation and increasing synaptic activity in the brain."

6   Dr. Nakamatsu eats just one regular meal a day, and he routinely photographs every dish before consuming it so that he can chart which meals most stimulate his creativity. He has even started his own line of snack foods, which he markets under the name Yummy Nutri Brain Food. Dr. Nakamatsu claims that these snacks "are very helpful to the brain's thinking process. They are a special mixture of dried shrimp, seaweed, cheese, yogurt, eel, eggs, beef, and chicken liver—all fortified with vitamins." He claims that his healthful lifestyle will allow him to live to be exactly 144 years old. It is not clear how he calculated his life span, but he is confident that he is accurate. He says he hopes to double the number of patents he holds before he dies in 2072.

7   Dr. Nakamatsu does all of his inventing at his house in Tokyo, where he has designed three special rooms to spark his creativity. One room, which he calls the "static room," is outfitted with a rock garden, natural running water, plants, stark white walls, and other natural elements to provide a calm and quiet environment for free thinking. Another room, which he calls the "dynamic room," is where he goes to refine his creative notions. It has black and white striped walls and is fully wired with electronic video and audio equipment, along with high-powered speakers that pump out jazz or his beloved Beethoven's Fifth. Finally, there is his pool room where Dr. Nakamatsu goes to sit underwater and hold his breath so that he can brainstorm creative new ideas. When he gets to his creative flash point, he jots down his ideas on a waterproof notepad.

8   Dr. Nakamatsu's formula for long-term success is simple: Don't work for other people and don't use other people's money. He has never sought funding from any person, corporation, or government. As he often says, "If you ask or borrow money from other people, you cannot keep freedom of intelligence."

9   Even though Dr. Nakamatsu already may hold the most patents in the world, he has no plans to retire. Why would he want to quit working? He's having the time of his life! Plus, he's still got quite a long time to live. "I enjoy every minute of my work 100 percent," he says. "I don't need relaxation because I relax all day." ✳

If you have been timed while reading this article, enter your reading time below. Then turn to the Words-per-Minute Table on page 147 and look up your reading speed (words per minute). Enter your reading speed on the graph on page 148.

Reading Time: Lesson 14

_____ : _____
Minutes   *Seconds*

A Finding the Main Idea

One statement below expresses the main idea of the article. One statement is too general, or too broad. The other statement explains only part of the article; it is too narrow. Label the statements using the following key:

M—Main Idea   **B—Too Broad**   **N—Too Narrow**

_____ 1. Dr. Nakamatsu has a unique creative style and has produced thousands of practical inventions.

_____ 2. Dr. Nakamatsu thought of his first invention when he was only five years old.

_____ 3. Dr. Nakamatsu is a highly creative and interesting man.

_____ Score 15 points for a correct M answer.

_____ Score 5 points for each correct B or N answer.

_____ **Total Score**: Finding the Main Idea

B Recalling Facts

How well do you remember the facts in the article? Put an X in the box next to the answer that correctly completes each statement about the article.

1. To Dr. Nakamatsu, "creative swimming" means
    ☐ a. swimming for fun with a team of assistants.
    ☐ b. staying underwater until the lack of oxygen triggers his creativity.
    ☐ c. thinking of new swimming strokes.

2. Dr. Nakamatsu invented what would become the first compact disc
    ☐ a. so he could hear music without distortion.
    ☐ b. to have a place to store computer files.
    ☐ c. to get a job at a big company.

3. Dr. Nakamatsu is working on a special house that is powered by
    ☐ a. energy from deep within the earth.
    ☐ b. cosmic energy.
    ☐ c. thought waves.

4. Dr. Nakamatsu's snack food brand is called
    ☐ a. Food for Creative Brainiacs.
    ☐ b. Delicious and Nutritious Brain Food.
    ☐ c. Yummy Nutri Brain Food.

5. Dr. Nakamatsu believes that he will live to the age of
    ☐ a. 144.
    ☐ b. 111.
    ☐ c. 172.

Score 5 points for each correct answer.

_____ **Total Score**: Recalling Facts

C Making Inferences

When you combine your own experiences and information from a text to draw a conclusion that is not directly stated in that text, you are making an inference. Below are five statements that may or may not be inferences based on information in the article. Label the statements using the following key:

C—Correct Inference **F—Faulty Inference**

_____ 1. Only mature adults can come up with truly creative and practical inventions.

_____ 2. Dr. Nakamatsu's underwater brainstorming method is dangerous.

_____ 3. Other than Dr. Nakamatsu, hardly anyone in Japan has invented anything.

_____ 4. Dr. Nakamatsu changes his lifestyle habits and creative methods very frequently.

_____ 5. Dr. Nakamatsu's goal is to invent things that fill a need, not necessarily to make a lot of money.

Score 5 points for each correct answer.

_____ **Total Score**: Making Inferences

D Using Words Precisely

Each numbered sentence below contains an underlined word or phrase from the article. Following the sentence are three definitions. One definition is closest to the meaning of the underlined word. One definition is opposite or nearly opposite. Label those two definitions using the following key. Do not label the remaining definition.

C—Closest **O—Opposite or Nearly Opposite**

1. Dr. Nakamatsu played his favorite Beethoven record so often that the music became <u>distorted</u> with hisses and scratches.

_____ a. distinct

_____ b. unclear

_____ c. familiar

2. His <u>prolific</u> career as an inventor has also earned him the unofficial title as "the Edison of Japan."

_____ a. very productive

_____ b. with little result

_____ c. long-lasting

3. He sleeps only four hours a night because he believes that sleeping more than six hours out of 24 <u>diminishes</u> brain power.

_____ a. increases

_____ b. reacts to

_____ c. shrinks

4. "Special sound frequencies pulse from the footrest to the headrest, <u>stimulating</u> blood circulation and increasing synaptic activity in the brain."

_____ a. showing

_____ b. blocking

_____ c. making active, moving

5. The second room, which he calls the "dynamic room," is where he goes to <u>refine</u> his creative notions.

_____ a. improve by making small changes

_____ b. consider seriously

_____ c. make worse bit by bit

_____ Score 3 points for each correct C answer.

_____ Score 2 points for each correct O answer.

_____ **Total Score**: Using Words Precisely

Enter the four total scores in the spaces below, and add them together to find your Reading Comprehension Score. Then record your score on the graph on page 149.

Score	Question Type	Lesson 14
_____	Finding the Main Idea	
_____	Recalling Facts	
_____	Making Inferences	
_____	Using Words Precisely	
_____	**Reading Comprehension Score**	

Author's Approach

Put an X in the box next to the correct answer.

1. The main purpose of the first paragraph is to
☐ a. list Dr. Nakamatsu's inventions.
☐ b. compare Dr. Nakamatsu with other inventors.
☐ c. stress how unusual Dr. Nakamatsu's creative process is.

2. What is the author's purpose in writing this article?
☐ a. to encourage the reader to invent things
☐ b. to inform the reader about an interesting, creative person
☐ c. to express an opinion about creative people

3. Choose the statement below that best describes the author's position in paragraph 5.
☐ a. Dr. Nakamatsu lives life in quite a unique way.
☐ b. Dr. Nakamatsu's lifestyle is not out of the ordinary.
☐ c. Dr. Nakamatsu should try to be a little more normal.

4. What does the author imply by saying "But maybe the order should be reversed; maybe Thomas Edison should be called 'the Dr. NakaMats of the United States'"?
☐ a. Most people don't know the difference between Dr. Nakamatsu and Thomas Edison.
☐ b. Thomas Edison might be a greater inventor than Dr. Nakamatsu.
☐ c. Dr. Nakamatsu might be a greater inventor than Thomas Edison.

_____ Number of correct answers

Record your personal assessment of your work on the Critical Thinking Chart on page 150.

CRITICAL THINKING

Summarizing and Paraphrasing

Put an X in the box next to the correct answer.

1. Read the statement from the article below. Then read the paraphrase of that statement. Choose the reason that best tells why the paraphrase does not say the same thing as the statement.

   Statement: Dr. Nakamatsu eats just one regular meal a day, and he routinely photographs every dish before consuming it so that he can chart which meals most stimulate his creativity.

   Paraphrase: Dr. Nakamatsu eats only one meal a day, and he keeps a record of what he has eaten so that he can chart which meals made him most creative.

   ☐ a. Paraphrase says too much.
   ☐ b. Paraphrase doesn't say enough.
   ☐ c. Paraphrase doesn't agree with the statement.

2. Below are summaries of the article. Choose the summary that says all the most important things about the article but in the fewest words.

   ☐ a. Dr. Nakamatsu, an interesting person with a unique lifestyle, employs some unusual creative methods to invent a number of useful products.

   ☐ b. Dr. Nakamatsu was born in 1928 in Japan and has lived such a productive life since then that he is often called the "Thomas Edison of Japan."

   ☐ c. Dr. Nakamatsu has given the world thousands of useful products, such as the CD, the DVD, the Cerebrex chair, the digital watch, and the taxicab meter.

> _____ Number of correct answers
>
> Record your personal assessment of your work on the Critical Thinking Chart on page 150.

Critical Thinking

Put an X in the box next to the correct answer for questions 1, 2, and 5. Follow the directions provided for the other questions.

1. Which of the following statements from the article is an opinion rather than a fact?

   ☐ a. Dr. Nakamatsu has never sought funding from any person, corporation, or government.

   ☐ b. If you ask or borrow money from other people, you cannot keep freedom of intelligence.

   ☐ c. Dr. Nakamatsu does his inventing at his house in Tokyo, where he has designed three different rooms to spark his creativity.

2. From the article, you can predict that

   ☐ a. Dr. Nakamatsu will find out that he can be just as creative while living a quiet, normal lifestyle.

   ☐ b. Dr. Nakamatsu will continue to think up new inventions.

   ☐ c. Dr. Nakamatsu will go to work for the Japanese government.

3. Choose from the letters below to correctly complete the following statement. Write the letter on the lines.

   On the positive side, _____, but on the negative side, _____.

   a. Dr. Nakamatsu's creative swimming process works well for him

   b. Dr. Nakamatsu's creative swimming process takes place in a special room in his house in Tokyo

   c. Dr. Nakamatsu's creative swimming process could accidentally lead to trouble

CRITICAL THINKING

4. Reread paragraph 4. Then choose from the letters below to correctly complete the following statement. Write the letters on the lines.

According to paragraph 5, _____ because _____.

a. the Cerebrex chair increases brain activity

b. Dr. Nakamatsu believes too much sleep diminishes his brain power

c. Dr. Nakamatsu doesn't sleep much

5. What did you have to do to answer question 4?

☐ a. find a cause (why something happened)

☐ b. find an opinion (what someone thinks about something)

☐ c. find a contrast (how things are different)

_____ Number of correct answers

Record your personal assessment of your work on the Critical Thinking Chart on page 150.

Personal Response

How do you think you would feel if someone like Dr. Nakamatsu lived with you and your family?

_____

_____

_____

_____

Self-Assessment

I'm proud of how I answered question _____ in section _____ because

_____

_____

_____

_____

_____

_____

_____

_____

CRITICAL THINKING

Sign of the Times

José Hernandez-Rebollar demonstrates his AcceleGlove, which can translate hand movements into spoken words or text.

I n 2000 José Hernandez-Rebollar was studying electrical engineering at George Washington University in Washington, D.C. He was a brilliant student, and he was determined to combine his passion for electronics with his desire to help others. Hernandez-Rebollar wanted to create an innovative product that used motion-control technology to translate American Sign Language (ASL) into spoken and written English. ASL has been around nearly 200 years, "yet unlike most other languages, we do not have electronic translation for ASL," Hernandez-Rebollar explained. He had no experience working with the deaf or with sign language, but he was confident he could learn enough about them to create a useful product. Hernandez-Rebollar eventually did create a wonderful device, but the reaction to it wasn't exactly what he expected.

2   José Hernandez-Rebollar grew up in the Mexican state of Puebla and completed most of his schooling there. He chose to study electrical engineering in college because he loved to experiment. He joked that he considered becoming a doctor but changed his mind because "in electrical engineering if I blow up something, I can buy another one and it's no problem." While studying at the University of Puebla,

he also began working at a science research institute in Tonantzintla. From here, he became involved in designing the largest radio telescope in the world, which would be built on Sierra Negra, one of the many mountain peaks surrounding Puebla. Hernandez-Rebollar's main duties included working on the computer controls for the telescope's antenna.

3   Hernandez-Rebollar's supervisors were so impressed with him that they urged him to apply for a Fulbright scholarship. Money from this prestigious scholarship would allow Hernandez-Rebollar to complete his engineering studies in the United States. He also would be able to work on his visionary ASL translation project.

4   Hernandez-Rebollar firmly believed his motion-control translation idea would be something that deaf people could use every day and in any situation. There are about 28 million people in the United States with some degree of hearing loss. Most are able to use hearing aids, which amplify sound so that users can continue to understand the human voice. Some people, however, have no hearing at all. They must communicate through sign language using their hands. Between 500,000 and 2 million Americans communicate through American Sign Language. That makes it one of the most commonly used languages in the country. Until recently, however, the only way for a deaf person using ASL to communicate with a hearing person has been by using an interpreter, a hearing person who

can translate ASL into spoken words. Hernandez-Rebollar hoped his translating device would reduce or even eliminate the need for human translators.

5   In 1998 Hernandez-Rebollar won his Fulbright and moved to Washington, D.C., to begin working on a Ph.D., a high-level degree, in electrical engineering at George Washington University. His move from Mexico to the U.S. capital was not an easy

switch. His English was inadequate, and he knew very little about American culture. He struggled at first, but with determination he found a way to work on his school studies, his research, and also learn English. In 2003 Hernandez-Rebollar received his Ph.D.

6   Another result of his long years of study and hard work was the completion of his project. He called it the AcceleGlove—a sensor-studded electronic glove that uses

Individual finger movements command the functions of this robot.

motion-control technology to translate sign language gestures into spoken words or text. Here's how it works: The user puts on the glove, which has straps around the wrist and up on the arm. When the user makes a sign in ASL, the glove's built-in microcomputer maps the movement of the fingers, hand, and arm and translates the sign into speech or text. Within a millisecond of any gesture, the word or phrase is recognized and spoken as a computerized voice through an amplifier or displayed on a monitor.

7   The AcceleGlove did have some limitations for ASL. For one thing, it was not 100 percent accurate. For "easy" words or letters, it scored in the high 90 percent range, but for "hard" words the accuracy range dropped into the 60 to 70 percent range. Also, since there was only one glove, the number of possible words and phrases was limited to those that can be signed with one hand. ASL has a few hundred one-hand words and some important one-hand expressions, such as "What's the matter?" and "I'll help you." There also are many complex phrases that require both hands as well as facial expressions. Still, all the letters of the alphabet could be made with one hand, so it was possible to spell out any word or phrase with the AcceleGlove. Upgrades in the technology may solve some of these problems. Changes already have been made so that the glove can be programmed to translate ASL into Spanish.

8   The biggest problem Hernandez-Rebollar still faces with the AcceleGlove is getting the deaf community to accept it. The lack of 100 percent accuracy makes some potential users distrust the glove, fearing it will lead to miscommunication. More importantly, some people in the deaf community say they don't want to use the glove no matter how well it works. For many deaf people, using ASL is part of their unique culture. They want the hearing world to accept deaf people rather than force deaf people to use technology to accommodate the hearing world. Paul Mitchell, director of the American Sign Language Institute, says, "I think the tendency in deaf culture is to use natural signing and human interpreters." Still, there are some in the deaf community who welcome Hernandez-Rebollar's technology. Corinne Vinopol, the head of the Institute for Disabilities, Research, and Training, Inc., thinks the glove would be especially useful in families with deaf parents and hearing children or vice versa. When the glove is perfected, it can also be used to teach ASL.

9   Other institutions have welcomed the AcceleGlove with open arms. Automobile manufactures and medical-technology industries, for example, use robotics to perform many important tasks. Robot arms can be controlled with the AcceleGlove's hand and finger motions to install parts on an assembly line or perform delicate surgery in an operating room or a doctor's office. The glove also can be modified for use by public safety, emergency, or military personnel in situations where silent communication with a command center over short or long distance is necessary.

10   José Hernandez-Rebollar's experience with the deaf community may provide a lesson for those who are looking to build the next big thing. Just because you think your technology will fill the needs of a particular population does not necessarily mean that the population will welcome or adopt it. In the end, it is the people who use the technology who decide how the technology is used. ✷

If you have been timed while reading this article, enter your reading time below. Then turn to the Words-per-Minute Table on page 147 and look up your reading speed (words per minute). Enter your reading speed on the graph on page 148.

Reading Time: Lesson 15

_____ : _____
Minutes   *Seconds*

A Finding the Main Idea

One statement below expresses the main idea of the article. One statement is too general, or too broad. The other statement explains only part of the article; it is too narrow. Label the statements using the following key:

M—Main Idea   **B—Too Broad**   **N—Too Narrow**

_____ 1. Research is being done to find ways to help hearing people and deaf people who use sign language to communicate.

_____ 2. José Hernandez-Rebollar invented an electronic glove that translates sign language into spoken words or text.

_____ 3. José Hernandez-Rebollar moved from Mexico to study at George Washington University in Washington, D.C.

_____ Score 15 points for a correct M answer.

_____ Score 5 points for each correct B or N answer.

_____ **Total Score**: Finding the Main Idea

B Recalling Facts

How well do you remember the facts in the article? Put an X in the box next to the answer that correctly completes each statement about the article.

1. In Mexico, Hernandez-Rebollar worked
☐ a. as a doctor.
☐ b. on the computer controls for a large telescope.
☐ c. as an electrical engineer.

2. The number of people in the United States with some hearing loss is estimated to be
☐ a. 500,000.
☐ b. 2 million.
☐ c. 28 million.

3. The AcceleGlove
☐ a. uses motion-control to translate sign language.
☐ b. uses robot arms to perform sign language.
☐ c. speaks in limited words and phrases.

4. Some in the deaf community do not accept the AcceleGlove because
☐ a. it is slow.
☐ b. it is heavy.
☐ c. it is not 100 percent accurate.

5. The AcceleGlove has been welcomed by
☐ a. medical-technology industries.
☐ b. agricultural workers.
☐ c. physical therapists.

Score 5 points for each correct answer.

_____ **Total Score**: Recalling Facts

C Making Inferences

When you combine your own experiences and information from a text to draw a conclusion that is not directly stated in that text, you are making an inference. Below are five statements that may or may not be inferences based on information in the article. Label the statements using the following key:

C—Correct Inference   **F—Faulty Inference**

_____ 1. Many deaf people think hearing people should learn American Sign Language.

_____ 2. Hernandez-Rebollar did not seek advice from the deaf community when he developed the AcceleGlove.

_____ 3. American Sign Language is very difficult to learn.

_____ 4. The deaf community is proud of its culture.

_____ 5. The AcceleGlove, as an aid to deaf people, is a total failure.

Score 5 points for each correct answer. _____ **Total Score**: Making Inferences

D Using Words Precisely

Each numbered sentence below contains an underlined word or phrase from the article. Following the sentence are three definitions. One definition is closest to the meaning of the underlined word. One definition is opposite or nearly opposite. Label those two definitions using the following key. Do not label the remaining definition.

C—Closest   **O—Opposite or Nearly Opposite**

1. Money from this <u>prestigious</u> scholarship would allow Hernandez-Rebollar to complete his engineering studies in the United States.

_____ a. honored; having a good reputation

_____ b. expensive

_____ c. not important

2. Most hearing-impaired people use hearing aids that <u>amplify</u> sounds.

_____ a. make greater, strengthen

_____ b. decrease

_____ c. distort or change

3. When Hernandez-Rebollar moved from Mexico, his English was <u>inadequate</u>.

_____ a. satisfactory

_____ b. confusing, baffling

_____ c. not good enough

4. They want the hearing world to accept deaf people rather than force deaf people to use technology to <u>accommodate</u> the hearing world.

_____ a. ignore or neglect

_____ b. adjust for; make changes to satisfy

_____ c. assist

5. Robot arms can perform <u>delicate</u> surgery.

_____ a. last-minute, emergency

_____ b. easy, uncomplicated

_____ c. difficult, requiring great care

_____ Score 3 points for each correct C answer.

_____ Score 2 points for each correct O answer.

_____ **Total Score**: Using Words Precisely

Enter the four total scores in the spaces below, and add them together to find your Reading Comprehension Score. Then record your score on the graph on page 149.

Score	Question Type	Lesson 15
_____	Finding the Main Idea	
_____	Recalling Facts	
_____	Making Inferences	
_____	Using Words Precisely	
_____	**Reading Comprehension Score**	

Author's Approach

Put an X in the box next to the correct answer.

1. Choose the statement below that best describes the author's opinion.

☐ a. Just because you think your technology will fill the needs of a particular population does not necessarily mean that population will welcome or adopt it.

☐ b. While the AcceleGlove may or may not be accepted by the ASL community someday, other institutions have welcomed it.

☐ c. The AcceleGlove has too many limitations to be useful.

2. Choose the statement below that best explains how the author addresses an opposing point of view about the development of the AcceleGlove.

☐ a. The AcceleGlove is not 100 percent accurate.

☐ b. When the glove is perfected, it can also be used to teach ASL.

☐ c. The ASL community wants the hearing world to accept deaf people rather than force deaf people to use technology to accommodate the hearing world.

3. The author probably wrote this article in order to

☐ a. describe the invention that uses motion-control technology for many helpful purposes.

☐ b. inform the reader about the deaf community.

☐ c. recognize the importance of American Sign Language.

_____ Number of correct answers

Record your personal assessment of your work on the Critical Thinking Chart on page 150.

CRITICAL THINKING

144

Summarizing and Paraphrasing

Put an X in the box next to the correct answer for questions 1 and 2. Follow the directions provided for question 3.

1. Below are summaries of the article. Choose the summary that says all the most important things about the article but in the fewest words.

☐ a. Hernandez-Rebollar worked for many years on an invention that he hoped would help people communicate.

☐ b. Hernandez-Rebollar invented the AcceleGlove while studying at George Washington University in Washington, D.C.

☐ c. The AcceleGlove was invented by Hernandez-Rebollar to translate sign language into speech. It has not been accepted by the entire deaf community, but other uses have been found.

2. Choose the sentence that correctly restates the following sentence from the article: "He chose to study electrical engineering in college because he loved to experiment."

☐ a. In college, he loved to carry out experiments in electrical engineering.

☐ b. He selected electrical engineering experiments in college.

☐ c. Since he loved experimenting, he decided to study electrical engineering at college.

3. Reread paragraph 8 in the article. Below, write a summary of the paragraph in no more than 15 words.

_____

_____

_____

_____

_____ Number of correct answers

Record your personal assessment of your work on the Critical Thinking Chart on page 150.

Critical Thinking

Put an X in the box next to the correct answer for questions 1, 2, 4, and 5. Follow the directions provided for question 3.

1. Which of the following statements from the article is an opinion rather than a fact?

☐ a. "For many deaf people, using ASL is part of their unique culture."

☐ b. "Hernandez-Rebollar grew up in the Mexican state of Puebla and completed most of his schooling there."

☐ c. "The glove would be especially useful in families with deaf parents and hearing children or vice versa."

2. From the article, you can predict that

☐ a. improvements will be made to the AcceleGlove.

☐ b. the deaf community will ban the use of the AcceleGlove.

☐ c. doctors will be replaced by robots using the AcceleGlove motion-control technology.

3. Choose from the letters below to correctly complete the following statement. Write the letters on the lines.

On the positive side, _____, but on the negative side, _____.

a. ASL is one of the most commonly used languages in the country

b. the AcceleGlove currently is limited to words that are signed with one hand

c. the AcceleGlove can translate sign language into speech

4. How is "Sign of the Times" an example of the theme of *Visionaries*?

☐ a. Hernandez-Rebollar applied existing technology to an invention that he believed would help people.

☐ b. Hernandez-Rebollar worked hard to develop the AcceleGlove.

☐ c. Hernandez-Rebollar struggled to adjust to American culture.

5. From the information in paragraph 8, you can conclude that

☐ a. deaf people distrust technology.

☐ b. Hernandez-Rebollar expected the deaf community to welcome the AcceleGlove.

☐ c. all deaf people would use the AcceleGlove if it were 100 percent accurate.

_____ Number of correct answers

Record your personal assessment of your work on the Critical Thinking Chart on page 150.

Personal Response

Would you recommend this article to other students? Why or why not.

_____

_____

_____

_____

_____

_____

_____

Self-Assessment

Which ideas from the article were difficult to understand?

_____

_____

_____

_____

_____

_____

_____

_____

Which were easy to understand?

_____

_____

_____

_____

_____

_____

_____

_____

Compare and Contrast

Think about the articles you have read in Unit Three. Choose three articles from which you learned the most. Write the titles of the articles in the first column of the chart below. Use information you learned from the articles to fill in the empty boxes in the chart.

Title	What qualities do you most admire in this visionary?	What surprised or disappointed you the most about this person?	What single lesson did you learn from this visionary?

Imagine you are about to begin working on a project with one of the visionaries you selected. What project would it be? Why do you think you would

be a good team? _____

_____

_____

_____ .

Words-per-Minute Table

Unit Three

Directions If you were timed while reading an article, refer to the Reading Time you recorded in the box at the end of the article. Use this words-per-minute table to determine your reading speed for that article. Then plot your reading speed on the graph on page 148.

Lesson	11	12	13	14	15	
No. of Words	1212	1204	1036	1059	1118	
1:30	808	803	691	706	745	90
1:40	727	722	622	635	671	100
1:50	661	657	565	578	610	110
2:00	606	602	518	530	559	120
2:10	559	556	478	489	516	130
2:20	519	516	444	454	479	140
2:30	485	482	414	424	447	150
2:40	455	452	389	397	419	160
2:50	428	425	366	374	395	170
3:00	404	401	345	353	373	180
3:10	383	380	327	334	353	190
3:20	364	361	311	318	335	200
3:30	346	344	296	303	319	210
3:40	331	328	283	289	305	220
3:50	316	314	270	276	292	230
4:00	303	301	259	265	280	240
4:10	291	289	249	254	268	250
4:20	280	278	239	244	258	260
4:30	269	268	230	235	248	270
4:40	260	258	222	227	240	280
4:50	251	249	214	219	231	290
5:00	242	241	207	212	224	300
5:10	235	233	201	205	216	310
5:20	227	226	194	199	210	320
5:30	220	219	188	193	203	330
5:40	214	212	183	187	197	340
5:50	208	206	178	182	192	350
6:00	202	201	173	177	186	360
6:10	197	195	168	172	181	370
6:20	191	190	164	167	177	380
6:30	186	185	159	163	172	390
6:40	182	181	155	159	168	400
6:50	177	176	152	155	164	410
7:00	173	172	148	151	160	420
7:10	169	168	145	148	156	430
7:20	165	164	141	144	152	440
7:30	162	161	138	141	149	450
7:40	158	157	135	138	146	460
7:50	155	154	132	135	143	470
8:00	152	151	130	132	140	480

Minutes and Seconds

Seconds

Plotting Your Progress: Reading Speed

Unit Three

Directions If you were timed while reading an article, write your words-per-minute rate for that article in the box under the number of the lesson. Then plot your reading speed on the graph by putting a small X on the line directly above the number of the lesson, across from the number of words per minute you read. As you mark your speed for each lesson, graph your progress by drawing a line to connect the Xs.

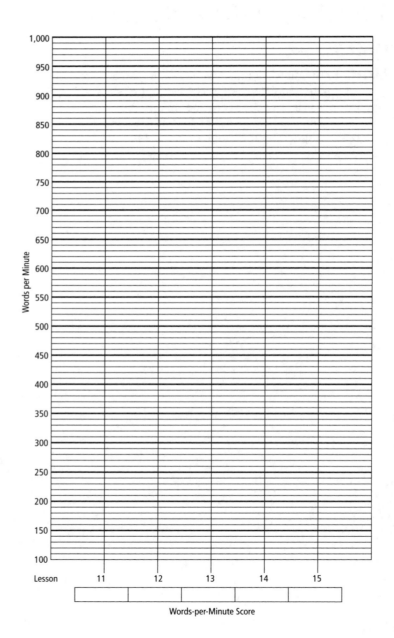

Words per Minute

Lesson 11 12 13 14 15

Words-per-Minute Score

Plotting Your Progress: Reading Comprehension

Unit Three

Directions Write your Reading Comprehension score for each lesson in the box under the number of the lesson. Then plot your score on the graph by putting a small X on the line directly above the number of the lesson and across from the score you earned. As you mark your score for each lesson, graph your progress by drawing a line to connect the Xs.

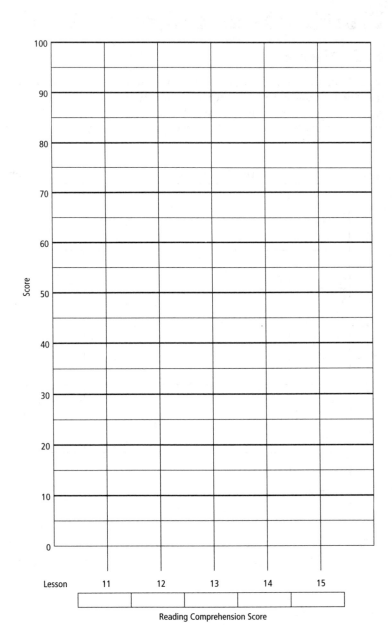

Score

Lesson 11 12 13 14 15

Reading Comprehension Score

Plotting Your Progress: Critical Thinking

Unit Three

Directions Work with your teacher to evaluate your responses to the Critical Thinking questions for each lesson. Then fill in the appropriate spaces in the chart below. For each lesson and each type of Critical Thinking question, do the following: Mark a minus sign (–) in the box to indicate areas in which you feel you could improve. Mark a plus sign (+) to indicate areas in which you feel you did well. Mark a minus-slash-plus sign (–/+) to indicate areas in which you had mixed success. Then write any comments you have about your performance, including ideas for improvement.

Lesson	Author's Approach	Summarizing and Paraphrasing	Critical Thinking
11			
12			
13			
14			
15			

Image Credits

Cover Robert Harding Picture Library/SuperStock; **4–5** The Granger Collection, New York; **14–15** Tom Rielly; **22–23** Lelli & Masotti/Alinari/Lebrecht; **30–31** Rosalie Winard; **38–39** Bettmann/CORBIS; **46** Mariella Lombard/NY Daily News; **47** Michael Branscom; **60** Spencer Arnold/Getty Images; **61** imagebroker.net/SuperStock; **68** WENN/Newscom; **69** AP Photo/Lee Jin-man; **76** Nina Leen/Time & Life Pictures/Getty Images; **77** Science & Behavior Books, Inc.; **84** Viviane Moos/CORBIS; **85** DOMINIC FAVRE/epa/CORBIS; **92** Rick Friedman/CORBIS; **93** Paul Burns/Riser/Getty Images; **106** David Howells/CORBIS; **107** Time Life Pictures/Department Of Defense (DOD)/Time Life Pictures/Getty Images; **114** Mansell/Time Life Pictures/Getty Images; **115** Fotosearch/Getty Images; **122** A.H.M REZWAN/AFP/Getty Images; **123** Ashden Awards for Sustaninable Energy.; **130** YURIKO NAKAO/Reuters/CORBIS; **131** YOSHIKAZU TSUNO/AFP/Getty Images; **138** LUKE FRAZZA/AFP/Getty Images; **139** AnthroTronix, Inc.